E. M. CREIGHTON

LOOKING BACK

First Published 1998

ISBN: 0-9532188-0-5

Published by
E. M. Creighton ©
Parkhill Cottage
Stockbridge
Peterhead
Aberdeenshire
AB42 3LE

Cover reproduced in oils by the Author
from a painting by
Joseph Farquaharson

Typeset in Times 10/14pt & Bonney 16pt by
G & M Services
Peterhead
Aberdeenshire

Printed and bound in Scotland by
P SCROGIE
Peterhead, Aberdeenshire

In *Looking Back*, E M Creighton paints us a vivid picture of her early life on a farm through the innocent and inquisitive eyes of a child, living in a community experiencing the hardship of the war years, when the spirit and humour of the North East people burned at its brightest. The reader is then treated to a light-hearted insight into the Author's post-war nursing life, her often eventful career as the owner of local boarding kennels and later, in a variety of roles, from fundraiser for the people of Bosnia, to a 'fearless kitten rescuer' for the Cats Protection League!

Looking Back is a moving and often amusing account of one woman's life in the North East of Scotland from 1929 to the present day. Yet through it all, is threaded the sadness of distressing childhood events, which return to cause her pain in late adulthood, a time when all her inner strength and dignity is required to get through the 'bad times' and achieve peace and contentment in later life.

Best wishes
E. M. Creighton

CONTENTS

PART 1 - CHILDHOOD MEMORIES

PART 2 - TO THE PRESENT DAY

Dedication

I dedicate this book to Willy.

*Without his support and encouragement,
this book would not have been written.*

Acknowledgements

I would like to give my grateful thanks to

*Margaret & Gill,
My 'ladies' from G & M Services
For their many, many hours of
dedicated hard work, without which,
this book may not have been printed.*

PART 1

CHILDHOOD MEMORIES

CHAPTER 1

IN THE BEGINNING

My father was a Marine Engineer, having served his apprenticeship, before the 1914 - 1918 war. During the first World War, he was with the Gordon Highlanders' but whilst fighting in France, he was wounded and had to return to Britain. After he recovered, he transferred to the Royal Flying Corps with whom he served till after the end of the war.

On demob, he could not get employment in this country and was negotiating for a job in India, but plans had to be abandoned at speed on the death of his father, at the age of fifty seven. He then had to take over the running of the farm, which at that time, he had no experience of.

My parents were married on 2nd June 1920 and moved into the big old rambling farmhouse. My two brothers were born in June 1921 and March 1925. Just before I joined the family it was decided to demolish the old farmhouse and replace it with a modern two storey house, to be built on the old site.

Meantime, the family would live in one of the farm cottages. During the building, a stone dated 1929 was built into the front of the house and I was born on 12th June of the same year.

I have been told that my mother caught an infection, which resulted in her developing a condition then called 'Child Bed Fever', now referred to as 'Puerperal Fever'. She spent twelve weeks in a private nursing home.

During that time, I was taken home and looked after by a proper baby nurse I have a photograph of this lady dressed in a long navy blue or dark coat and wearing a fancy flowing cap. I think her name was 'Nurse Brooks'. In the photograph, was a very old fashioned deep pram and I presume I was in there somewhere.

I don't know how long Nurse Brooks stayed in the household looking after me, but the new house, my mother's hospital fees and my nurses salary were all paid for by my paternal grandmother. She was a fairly well off widow who lived in a flat in town. My father could not have afforded that sort of expenses. After Nurse Brooks services were no longer required, a dear '*coothie*' lady called Miss Murray took on the task of 'rearing' me, she must have been aged about fifty at the time. She made herself available to families who had someone in the household who required nursing or care, in any shape or form.

She had no training whatsoever, but was brimming over with tender loving care. She looked after me, I gather, until I went to school at Easter at just under five years old. She really was 'My Mother' and I was known to her and her friends as 'My Bairn'. Everybody adored her, but I was her special 'One' and the feelings were mutual.

Our water supply on the farm was very hard and limy, so rain water was often heated in a large pot. Central heating in those days was rather primitive, but it did supply a towel rail in the bathroom and a radiator on the top landing which took the chill off the upstairs bedrooms, if the doors were left open. The heating was turned on in the evenings when the water was hot enough, and could also be used for baths etc.

I do not remember my mother ever bathing me at all, she may have done, but I have no recollection of any physical contact till I was about four plus. It was winter time, the evenings were dark and I was having my hair washed. Meanwhile, my dad was standing on top of household steps nearby filling radiators in the attic with rain water, as limy water was supposed to corrode copper pipes etc.

I hated getting my hair washed, perhaps because the green soft soap shampoo sometimes got into my eyes and nipped a bit. I had struggled and knocked over the steps, presumably leaving my poor dad stranded in the attic!

At this point, someone had looked out of the open curtained, seawards facing window, and horrors; the 'Steading' or Farm Buildings were ablaze - panic ensued, the flames were leaping high into the sky, fire engines and policemen were everywhere. Finding a plentiful water supply in rural areas, in the event of fire, is always a problem. Hoses had to be laid down to the river about a quarter of a mile away. The steading was extensively damaged, the fire spreading rapidly due to the quantity of dry straw stored in the buildings.

I am very fond of animals, so am glad to have no recollection of any being lost or injured in the fire. I assume they were either set free, or were in a different part of the steading, I hope so, as it would have upset me greatly if any had died.

The fire was started by our 'maid' who apparently had a delight in seeing flames or fires. I don't know if it was considered a medical condition or not. She was identified as the culprit by the smell of burnt straw on her coat. Poor girl, she had to serve a prison sentence.

Strangely, she paid us a visit sometime after her release.

When I was about four and a half, I remember accompanying my dad to a nearby fishing village, on top of a box cart laden with bags of 'Kerr's Pink' potatoes, cabbages - Savoy's of course in those days, and beautiful carrots, completely free of damage from the carrot-root fly, as they were grown on sandy ground. Our load was duly delivered to customers, sought out by an elderly fisherman who used to help my dad to hand weed the carrots.

We had to get home before it was dark with the horse and cart as we never had lights. I suppose I was well wrapped up against the cold winter winds as a walking horse didn't lead to a speedy journey, but I loved being with my dad and would never have complained.

Also, when I was about the same age, or perhaps a little younger, our retired shepherd came with a pony and 'trap' to collect me and take me to his home in a lodge, for the day. He and his wife retired there, after spending many years of his working life shepherding on our farm.

He was affectionately known to everybody in the district as 'The Old Shepherd'. So much so that when a teacher asked her primary class who 'The Good Shepherd' was, one little boy shot his hand up in the air and said 'The Old Shepherd'.

He had an Old English Sheepdog, complete with long coat, it was called Spot. In those days the 'Bob Tails' as they are sometimes referred to now, were working dogs. This dear old gentleman was of a short, stocky build and I remember had short legs. He had a moustache and wore glasses and he and his wife both lived into their nineties.

My dad would often work along with him perhaps repairing fences or whatever had to be done. I remember my dad recalling a saying of the shepherd who would stand back and look at what they had done and say; "We dinna ah come speed alike but we have been very industrious."

I was taken to school on my first day of a new adventure and was overjoyed when we were allowed to play with a fairly large rocking horse. This pleasure was however for one day only and the poor horse was again returned to a large cupboard. On the second day at school, I travelled alone by bus, and was met at the bus stop by my grandmothers maid who presumably accompanied me to school.

To begin with, I went to my granny's for my dinner, she lived half way between the bus stop and the school which was very convenient. On the third day, the maid was a little late, or the bus a little early, whichever way, I ran, using a different route and arrived at granny's alone, much to my delight, as from an early age I have been of an independent mind.

The infant teacher I had for two years at the primary school happened to be a cousin of my mother's and used to visit us in an 'Austin' car fairly regularly on a Saturday morning on route to visit other relations. I used to be somewhat in awe of this visit as the thought of my teacher visiting, even though she was a relative, scared me a bit.

This feeling had nothing to do with my attitude towards her in school as she was a very gentle and loveable lady. I had somewhat the same feeling of awe when the minister called, perhaps every child did in those days, I don't know. Certainly we were brought up to respect them.

Another figure who commanded respect was the local policeman, who paid us visits on a strong, double barred black bicycle. We were duty bound to inform the constabulary when we were dipping sheep, which was law, presumably issued by the government. Dipping was meant to kill any 'creepy crawlies' and treat any skin infection or disease like scab.

The policeman had also to call and inspect ricks at threshing time to see we had close netting wire around the area to stop rats escaping. The rats were duly dispatched by the farm dogs or with sticks wielded by the farm workers. The rats stood no chance, although a few mice might escape. The many farm cats then took over and stood like sentries, waiting for the mice to pop out into the light of day.

After arriving home from school by bus, the first thing I had to do was take off my school clothes and put on what was called 'The Old Clothes'. As I always wore kilts, the old one might have been getting on the short side, despite having adjustable bodices, or perhaps it had become torn and was mended. Anyway, the old clothes were put on and the next thing was out to play.

In the wintertime that normally meant playing amongst the straw in the steading, sometimes jumping from couples under the roof. This jumping act was called our circus act! We tried to make sure that we were unobserved by the farm men as they didn't approve of our games. If caught, we were told in no uncertain fashion;"How would you like your food trampled on!" Either myself or one of the farm workers children would say that we would not like it and back would come the reply; "Well neither does the beasts!"

During the winters of my younger years, we often had heavy snow that lay for some time, especially when we had severe frost at nights to harden it. We used to sledge frequently down steep braes which were trodden in ridges by the sheep walking single file while the ground was wet. When the braes were snow clad with frosty snow, this made for a rather bumpy ride, which tended to speed the sledge up a bit. The sledges were all home made affairs, the runners were wood covered, with about 1in wide strips of smooth metal. These were scoured with emery paper to shine and smooth the runners, enabling the sledge to go faster.

If the frost was very severe, the river would be frozen at both sides, but only once can I ever remember it being frozen from side to side. When the river was partially frozen, it was not unknown for us to land on it, the run down the hill being so fast, As no-body ever went through the ice, I suppose we were very lucky. On the other side of the farm, there were other hills suitable for sledging, but the drawback there, was that we had a long haul uphill to the top before we could sled down again.

Sometimes, when my maiden Aunt was staying with us, she would relive her youth and come with us. She enjoyed herself immensely, which was not surprising as she was gifted with a great sense of humour, full of fun and always young at heart. All her nieces and nephews loved her.

CHAPTER 2

THE PICTURE HIGH ON THE WALL

After the fire that had burned down about half the steading in the mid thirties, it was rebuilt in a more modern design by a wonderful man called Willie Robbie. It was constructed of concrete, by a method of shuttering and pillars. Some roofs were slated, others had sheets of corrugated iron, which proved a problem in severe gales as if any sheets were slack, they tended to lift.

This same gentleman, went home at nights, after working with concrete all day, and painted the now famous pictures of the 'Clydesdale horses in harness'. He must have had a steady hand, to paint all the intricate harness. His paintings are now much sought after. At the same time, a new stable was built. In those days, horses did most of the work in the fields as that era was prior to the arrival of the Fordson tractor, generally accepted as the first mechanised machinery to take up residence on the farm.

The number of horses used on a farm depended largely on the acreage involved. This was roughly two horses, referred to as a 'Pair', per 100 acres. Our new stable was built to accommodate four horses, or two pairs, but I can recall it only having three occupants at one time. They were, of course, Clydesdales, the heavy working horse breed. We had two geldings and a mare, who was called the 'orra beast', or the odd one out. Her time was spent doing the odd jobs about the farm, like carting turnips, shimming turnips, raking hay, and any jobs requiring one horse only.

The two geldings did the ploughing, pulled the mower and, in harvest time, the binder. They were naturally bigger and stronger than the mare. If there was a lot of work to be done, we would occasionally hire a fourth horse from a Carter to work along with the mare, so making a second pair.

They each had their own harness, as the collar in particular, had to fit the neck comfortably, otherwise it would chaff and cause a sore. The harness was not new, it had been well worn, but was kept in reasonable condition with regular cleaning and oiling, which kept it supple. The harness was hung up on special wooden pegs attached to each stall, so they wouldn't get mixed up.

I can recall from the age of about four, being lifted on to one of the horses backs, to get a free ride from the field to the stables. That was considered a real treat and was very thrilling, though from my child's eyes, the ground did seem a long way down. There was little more to hang onto bar a handful of mane, but the horses were so steady, we youngsters never came to any harm.

The middle horse in the stable, a gelding, couldn't, or wouldn't, lie down at night to sleep, so a strong, leather strap with chains at each end was attached to strong hooks at both sides of the end of his stall. He used to lean all of his weight onto the strap and rest and sleep in that position. I suppose in the summer time, when out at grass, he would have laid down on the grass. I don't know the reason why he wouldn't lie down in the stable, perhaps he didn't like the confined space of his stall.

Later on, one of the geldings was replaced due to old age, and a second mare was bought. She and the original mare each produced two foals at yearly intervals, which meant that a couple of years later, we had four foals, or, 'clips' as they were called, at one time. They were quite tame as they were handled constantly, being taken to and from the loose box to the field on a rein.

I don't remember seeing any of them being 'broken in', which means being trained for wearing harness, pulling carts and implements etc, so presume they must have been sold unbroken. Breaking in a horse is a specialist job and requires a great deal of patience and kindness.

Built into the stable wall under the window, was what was called, the 'Corn Kist', where the bruised corn was kept for the horses. It was closed with a metal fastener called a 'sneck'. When closed, there was no chance of mice or the odd rat getting in for a free meal. Horses were fed more frequently than cattle and had to be rested for at least an hour after having a feed. This helped to prevent a serious condition called 'Colic', or a twisted bowel, which in extreme cases, could prove fatal.

There is also a condition that was relatively common in the North East of Scotland, called Grass Sickness. Why this disease should affect this area, I don't think has ever been clearly established. The onset is quick, the illness short and, as far as I can recollect, always fatal. Several horses from one farm can be affected in the same year, usually in the spring time, though the disease is not thought to be infectious.

I believe a study of the nature and cause of Grass Sickness was being carried out in Edinburgh a couple of years ago. I don't know if any progress was made as far as a cure was concerned, or the result of the study.

The stable was the equivalent to two stories high, with several skylights which provided plenty of air and light. Despite the skylights, when you opened the door, particularly in the morning, you were nearly knocked down by the strong smell of ammonia.

The floor was laid with round or oval smooth stones from the rocky shore which were pressed and hammered down onto a concrete foundation. This surface saved the horses from sliding and perhaps falling. Though they always had plenty of straw bedding, the floor surface tended to collect the urine which ran through the straw, thus producing the strong aroma.

On one of the gable walls, hung a picture approximately four feet by two and a half. It was in an ornate gilt frame and wasn't glazed. Looking back, it was bound to be an oil on canvas. It was there for decades, and in its time collected a considerable amount of dust and cobwebs. The picture depicted the Houses of Parliament, or, maybe the House of Lords as there was quite a lot of red in the clothing and the seating. As I think back almost sixty years, I can't be more accurate about the contents of the picture.

I presume it was bought at a roup, probably for very little, but was not considered suitable for the house, or it might just have been on the big side. However, why it ended up being hung in the stable, I will never know, but it was never moved, until the stable was converted into a grain store upon the advance of agriculture to the combine harvester, when it was goodbye to the working horses.

CHAPTER 3

THE CATTLEMAN AND THE CLOCK

In the thirties, forties and fifties, cattle which were fed for slaughter, were usually housed in the byres. A single byre had stalls up only side of the long wall, as opposed to a dairy byre where the stalls were usually up both sides, with a broad passage up the middle for ease of access. The feeding, or store cattle, either heifers or castrated bullocks, were loosely chained by the neck and the chain, or 'Binnin', was fixed to a sliding bar allowing the cattle a fair bit of freedom to move.

The cleaning out and feeding had to be carried out manually in those days. The dung was piled onto a barrow, making it very heavy, then wheeled and pushed, to the 'Midden', usually up a narrow plank, where it was emptied. There it was stored and compacted until late spring, when the midden was emptied, again a heavy manual task.

The men wore leggings, usually leather, on top of their boots and covering the foot of their trousers, both to try and keep them clean and also to reduce wear and tear. The task of emptying the midden usually took about three weeks to complete and their working clothes stank to high heaven. The house folk were thankful when the midden was finally emptied as the smell invaded the house. This was strongest at dinner times as the menfolk didn't remove their smelly clothing beforehand, there wasn't time. The unpleasant fragrance lingered in the house for some time, made worse by the hot stove in the kitchen.

Once the cattle had been cleaned out, they were bedded down with fresh, dry, golden straw, nothing like the musty baled straw that was stored out doors, as is frequently the case these days. The cattle were fed swede, turnip, hay or straw, drinking water being carried in large galvanised pails from a large round trough at the head of the byre.

Finally, the passage, or 'Greep', was swept with a heavy bristle brush. By now, the cattle were eating happily and would then settle down on a comfortable bed of straw. The byre looked very clean and as 'Neat as ninepence'.

The last task of the cattleman was to milk the one or two cows, depending on the time of year. The cows calved once a year, in spring or autumn, so we always had milk for ourselves and the farm workers families. Each family was given three pints a day as part of the wages, or perquisite, as it was called.

Waiting patiently in the passage, by the milk cows, sat the numerous farm cats, perhaps at times, three generations of them. They were waiting for their twice daily pudding dish of warm milk fresh from the cow. Years later, I learned that milk was one of the worst things to feed a cat, but then of course, in those days, there was no tinned cat food or its equivalent.

They got left overs of bread, porridge, potatoes, milk pudding and also hunted for mice and birds. Cats are much better catered for to-day, although these ones seemed to enjoy their treat, as they waited with great anticipation while the cows were being milked.

In the byre, above the door leading to the turnip, or 'Neep' shed, hung a rather nice wooden clock, with a round, white enamel dial and a box bit underneath. This clock kept good time and was religiously wound up by the cattleman. I suppose, like the picture in the stable, it had come from a 'Roup', or country auction. I used to think the picture and the clock were both rather grand for a steading.

CHAPTER 4

A YEAR IN THE LIFE OF A SHEEP

Somehow, sheep have always fascinated me, why I can't really say. They are not coloured like cattle for instance, and generally are all of similar size and shapes for their age. Their faces look similar, except to shepherds, who all claim they can identify each individual sheep. They also say they can tell which lambs the sheep had the previous year, their age, who their mothers were, etc. I must say, most of the faces of the same breed look quite alike to me, but then I'm not a shepherd.

Sheep are not credited with much in the way of brains, having a tendency to follow the leader, often in the wrong direction, much to the annoyance of the exasperated shepherd, especially if he is trying to train a young, inexperienced dog.

If one sheep finds a hole in a fence, it is soon joined by a number of friends, they then may land in a field of grain, which does harm both to the crop and the sheep's tummies!

Cattle, having four stomachs, fare worse as fermentation takes place, so bloating the beasts. This has sometimes to be treated by sticking a sharp, pointed, round metal spike right into the cows gut to release the gas. This instrument is called a 'Trocar and Canula'. The practice may seem brutal, but it gave immediate relief to the suffering animal.

The sheep season really begins in late autumn, in our case, the 1st of November, when the boys are introduced to the girls, as it were. The boys, or 'Tups', chests were painted a distinct colour, usually red or blue which was easily seen. A substance called 'Keel' was used, which did not harm the fleece. When they mated with the sheep, or 'Ewes', some of this keel was transferred to the rear ends of the sheep, so the shepherd then knew at a glance which of the sheep had been in season and successfully 'Served', as the expression is, or was.

These sheep were then expected to start lambing on, or after the 1st of April. The sheep that weren't in lamb, were usually fattened up and sold for meat, as it was not considered economical to hold on to them for another year.

The bigger the flock, the less sentiment and more viability. A flock numbered approximately four hundred and that number was a full time job for one shepherd. He was generally responsible for keeping the fences and gates in order as well as tending the sheep, so sometimes, he had help with fencing tasks, etc.

Depending on the temperature, the weather and the food supply, extra feed was generally given to the pregnant ewes, about six weeks before lambing. The aim of this was to produce good sized lambs and also helped the milk supply of the ewes after lambing. A lamb will soon suffer from hypothermia and dehydration in a cold April, if it doesn't have enough rich milk in its stomach. Ewes with no milk were no use in a flock, as the lambs then had to be fed with cows milk from a bottle, which is much less efficient and very time consuming.

Often, if the weather is frosty, cold and windy, the green grass becomes frost-burned, turns brown and disappears, which is disastrous. Turnips have then to be cut up and carted out to the ewes, along with any hay or a grain mix, to help them through the lean spell.

During the lambing, which lasts approximately a month, the shepherd and a helper slept in a hut, or similar accommodation, where they are able to observe the flock twenty four hours a day. The hut contained a stove for heating milk and also provided heat, both for the men and any weakly lambs, if chilled. There was provision for sleeping, tea making and the ever essential medicine chest, every shepherd had his own special medicines. Whilst not always kept very tidy, the hut was serviceable.

The in-lamb ewes were gathered in pens near the hut and lighting was set up so that the attendants could see all that was going on, or should be going on! Ewes frequently required a lot of assistance with lambing and single accommodation was available, so that the ewe could settle down with her new lamb, or lambs, in peace and comfort. Next morning, if all had went well, they were led into a nearby field. They were then checked regularly to make sure the ewes milk supply was adequate for the lambs and that the new-born were able to suckle.

It was also important to make sure that the lambs were with their correct mother, or for that matter, a mother at all. Sometimes, if a ewe had triplets for example, she may have insufficient milk to feed all three, also on occasion, a ewe did die while giving birth.

If another 'Foster' ewe was not available on these occasions, then the wee babes would be bottle fed with cows milk. This was a task usually assigned to us youngsters and much enjoyed, as the lambs were so adorable and used to follow us at feeding times, well, like lambs!

If another ewe had had only one lamb which for some reason had died, the shepherd would skin this lamb and put its skin over a weakly lamb, perhaps from a set of triplets. The skin would be just like a small coat and by doing this, it was hoped that the ewe would smell the skin of her own lamb and hopefully, once they got aquainted, would accept the youngster as her own.

That way, the small triplet would have a far better

chance of survival than if it had been left to compete with its other two siblings, who were usually bigger and stronger.

Sheep, like cattle, are influenced by the weather in many ways, windy weather makes them a bit high and excitable, while the approach of thunder has them racing about the field, perhaps they are affected by atmospheric pressure. At lambing time, if the ground is wet and it is raining heavily, it appears to encourage the sheep to give birth.

Whether it is again, atmospherics or perhaps, the suction of the wet ground, I don't know, but the shepherd will know to expect a busy night, and a good soaking! As a midwife, many years later, I always found that more babies were born during the night than the day time, it certainly seemed that way anyway, after a busy night shift.

When the lambing was finished, and the lambs old enough, or, as country folk described it; 'Well on their feet', the next procedure was for the males to be castrated and both sexes would have their tails docked, or cut. As far as I can recollect, black faced lambs didn't have to suffer the pain and indignity of the tail cutting, I believe it was something to do with the fact that they were grazed on high ground, which is far less intensive.

Lowland grazing was always heavier stocked, so tending to harbour the eggs and larvae of worms which built up in the gut of the sheep and lambs. This caused their bottoms and tail ends to become 'mucked-up' which attracted maggots. By cutting tails shorter than nature intended, it helped to keep bottoms clean and so deter the unwanted visitors.

Some time later, a liquid worm drench was invented which, when given in the correct dose and poured down the lambs throats at regular intervals, helped eradicate the problem, or at least, kept it at a manageable level.

The next major event in the sheep's calendar, was being bathed, or in sheep terms, 'Dipped'. There were special structures built of concrete for this purpose, with a sunken trough which had a gradual slope up out of one end. Heading into a deeper end, were tapering sheep pens with a two-way gate system. A similar pen arrangement led out of the sloping end, which had a concrete floor with grooves, designed so that the water ran back into the apex, like a draining board.

As the sheep were totally submerged while being dipped, they used to shake themselves vigorously when arriving onto dry land, showering water everywhere, hence the grooved floor. Once a particular batch was done, they were returned to the field, looking a decidedly dirty shade of yellow.

The liquid sheep dip came in drums, made by a veterinary firm called Coopers, which was very well known. It was diluted to instructed specifications, using warm water heated in a special boiler. The water was never really hot as the cold concrete absorbed some of the heat.

There were various dips to be used at different times of the year for different conditions, Scab and Maggots, for example. The shepherd wore a long apron and jacket, both waterproof, and wellington boots.

Some of the chemicals used on animals, have been banned, as have some used in horticulture and farming in general. There is great controversy over sheep dip containing Organo Phosphate at the present time. Some farmers, shepherds and market attendants are claiming they have suffered serious side-effects similar to those of sufferers of Myalgic Encephalomyelitis, or ME, leaving them permanently disabled. This chemical was also used in the manufacture of flea collars for cats, but is now banned, for that use anyway.

There is an alternative chemical for sheep dip, but, and there is always a but, it is not so effective! Therefore, certain farmers will continue to use the original, as they think better the product we know. The manufacturers maintain, that if it is used as directed, and with care, it is safe?

Shearing is another yearly task, which the ewes have to endure or enjoy, only a sheep would know. This is usually done at the end of May or beginning of June, depending on the weather. If the days were warm, the sheep felt the heat and would start rubbing themselves on the fences, perhaps they got itchy. Certainly their fleeces began to look loose and straggly and it was time they were removed, on the other hand, the sheep appeared quite keen to hold on to them.

Reluctant or not, they were gathered in, usually one field at a time if they were lowland grazed, while hill sheep were brought down as an entire flock. These sheep can sometimes belong to several owners, and the gathering may be a joint effort. Each sheep is individually marked with keel, in an individual area, colour and letter for each owner, eg Wilson may be; a red W painted on a left shoulder.

Once the sheep were gathered and herded into pens, or small paddock areas and provided the fleeces were dry, (it was also preferable that the sun be shining, as this helped the wool to rise), the process would begin.

The shearers were either the farm hands, or, if large numbers were involved, sometimes contractors were employed. These professional teams of shearers were often Australian or New Zealanders, who travelled the world from country to country, as the season progressed northwards.

One person caught the ewe and brought it, often half carrying the animal, to the shearer, who would sit the sheep smartly on its behind. He started on one side of its neck, and in a semi-circular sweeping motion, worked down towards the tail, from belly to back, or left to right. The sheep was then flipped over onto the clipped hip and the other side done in the same order. Any odd bits that were left were then tidied up, but a good shearer could normally remove the fleece in one piece.

The sheep was then re-marked with keel and released, normally bleating and looking for its lamb, or lambs. Once re-united with her offspring, the ewe was content. Sheep were either clipped with a set of hand shears, with broad blades, or, if electricity was at hand, by the more modern electric clippers, which had a two to two and a half inch blade.

A third person would then take over and gather up the fleece, spreading it out on a large sheet of canvas tarpaulin, before folding it in a specific way, so that the ends were turned and twisted then used to 'tie' the fleece into a neat parcel. The fleeces were then packed into really large sacks, and the top sewn with a large curved steel needle and strong twine.

A wool broker would then buy the wool and remove it by lorry for delivery to a mill where it was paid for by weight and quality. Various kinds of sheep have different textures of wool, so naturally the end products differ, and dictate whether the fleece was used to make, carpets, blankets, tweed, knitting wool etc.

That then is roughly a year in the life of a sheep, except for when the young ones were sold to new owners, or fattened for slaughter. Before I leave the 'Sheep to safely graze', I would like to ask the reader a question, "Did you ever wonder why lots of elderly shepherds will boast they still have their own teeth, instead of dentures?" Well, they would stoutly maintain, that is because they used their teeth to castrate male lambs, before spitting out the testicles!!

The working sheepdogs, ever in attendance, wasted no time in consuming these 'delicacies'. That was probably the only day of the year they tasted meat, raw meat! It must have been like Christmas day to the dogs, although I'm sure, not so for the poor lambs!

CHAPTER 5

BETWEEN SEASONS

Depending on the weather and the progress of crops, there was usually a couple of weeks available between the turnips and making hay, or, after the hay was safely ricked and before harvest time, for other jobs around the farm.

This time was spent tidying the steading and the ground surrounding the buildings. The men would 'Sheil', or scrape the weeds, nettles, docks and dandelions, which were then taken away by horse and cart and tipped into a dry ditch to fill up the ground.

The steading walls would be white washed, using a deep drum with a pump attached, which was on wheels and pushed with handles like those on a barrow.

Doors and windows would be painted and the whole place looked very clean and tidy. Sometimes, tools and implements would also be cleaned and painted. All this was done with usually six men, as opposed to to-day, when one man and perhaps contractors for harvesting etc, manage to do everything.

Things have changed so much on farms, it is very seldom nowadays, you see as we did, hens scraping a living around the yard, ducks scooping water up from puddles closely watched by the black and white collie dog. Eggs were usually plentiful and the odd fat hen would find its way into the pot at weekends. Hens didn't lay all the year round then as they were not intensively reared, as they are now.

They tended to be in full lay at Easter time, hence the 'Easter Eggs'. After a spell in full lay, they naturally went broody, especially the breeds like 'Light Sussex' and 'Rhode Island Reds'. They were called 'Cloaking Hens' and fertile eggs were placed under them to hatch out into chickens, ducks or turkeys, depending on the requirement at the time.

The hens felt very warm to the touch as if in a fever and shed their feathers, or moulted as it was called. As the chicks matured, the hens protected them by sitting loosely on top of them, and they in turn, would tuck themselves under the hens feathers. As the chickens got bigger, they grew their own feathers and mum would then start laying eggs again, having completed the cycle.

Nature, if left alone, is wonderful. It is when we, the clever ones, especially the scientists, start interfering in an effort to make animals more productive and therefore more profitable, that things start to go wrong. Sometimes very wrong, in my opinion.

By the time the young chickens were five to six

months old, roughly October, the pullets, or female chickens were themselves thinking about starting to lay, and they had the habit of finding hiding places in which to do so. A popular place on the farm was towards the top of the ricks of corn, or barley, newly built in the courtyard, as the harvest was now gathered in. The tops of the ricks were either thatched, or tied down with rough ropes or 'Rape', as they were called.

These ropes were hand made, often in the winter time on a really wet day, when little out-door work was possible, or desirable. They were made by two men, one at each end of thick strands of rough, softish twine, which was hooked on to three hooks attached to a piece of wood, a small handle like the starting handle of a car, would then be turned, causing the rope to twist. To attach this rope to the rick, a handful of the bottom of a sheaf would be twisted round to form a sort of knot, leaving an indentation in the rick.

This is where the pullets would frequently choose to lay and in order to collect the lovely brown, shiny fresh eggs, I had to get hold of a ladder, which was long, wooden and very heavy, then climb on to the rick, holding a basket with my other hand. It was a very satisfying job.

Less pleasant, was wading into the middle of a clump of nettles to retrieve the eggs, so cleverly hidden. Afterwards, your arms and legs were in no doubt as to where they had been, as there were no trousers worn by girls in those days!

Bringing home the harvest was, weather permitting, very congenial work. The grain smelt so fresh and looked so colourful, all golden and rustling. In the early days, the horses were used to cut the grain, pulling the binder which flung each individual sheaf out to the side in a neat row, so that it didn't get in the way the next time around. There was an iron seat on the binder from where the operator observed the proceedings and could assist, if necessary, the feed of the growing crop over the cutting blade.

A long wooden rake-like tool called a 'Tilter' was used for this task, which was needed if the crop was leaning away in the wrong direction, due to heavy rains or winds. If there were badly flattened areas, or a strip of grain growing close to the edge of the field, this had to be cut manually using a long, broad curved blade, attached to a long handle, this was called a 'Scythe'. To be effective, this task had to be performed in a rhythmic manner and though back breaking, was considered by many, to be satisfying and pleasant work.

The sheaves were gathered up, one under each arm, and set down with the stubble end on the ground. Eight sheaves were placed together to form an elegant upside down V shape. There was an art to building the 'Stooks' as they were called, so that if it rained, the water would run off instead of penetrating the centre of the stook. If that happened, on the first dry day following the rain, they had to be rebuilt, by turning them inside out, this job tended to soak the legs of the men.

It was important that the stooks were built in neat rows, this was not just for appearances sake, as later, when they became dry enough to be loaded on to carts, with special racks fitted to transport the grain to the cornyard, a straight line was easier to negotiate than if the stooks were dotted all over the place, which wasted precious time.

During seasonal work, like haymaking or harvesting, refreshments were taken to the field for the workers. I think generally this custom more or less began in wartime, when it was considered that the meals were perhaps, not very substantial and energy levels needed topping up between times. It was also started in towns within the factories, so heralding the birth of the tea break.

On our farm, a large brown enamel flagon, with a white interior and a sling handle, was wrapped up carefully with lots of layers of brown paper, then tied securely with string to keep the contents warm. This was filled with freshly made, fairly strong tea, which was well sugared, before creamy milk was added. Too bad if the men didn't like it that way, however, most did.

The hot tea was drank to wash down thick, double slices of bread and jam, or syrup, depending on which was available, as these were rationed. There was little sugar available to make home-made jam, unless you happened to keep bees, then you got an allowance for them. You could always try asking the bees nicely if they could spare a pound or two of their winter feed, the sugar, to make jam with!

At other times, scones or pancakes were made in the afternoons and despatched to the field, still warm from the girdle and wrapped in a clean towel. They were always popular and appreciated by the workers. The teas and 'eats' were carried to the field at 3pm, prompt. Farm folk were always keen on punctuality as far as meals were concerned, that was an unwritten rule.

Depending on where the harvest fields were, you had sometimes to carry the refreshments quite a distance, but there was never a complaint as the afternoons at harvest time would always be dry and sunny, otherwise the harvest would not be taking place, and at least the basket was considerably lighter in weight on the long walk home!

AUTUMN

Autumn is a favourite season
When everything is aglow
Field's are warm and golden
And the trees are on the blow

Gone are the days now
When nature gets a rest
To-day comes in the plough
And the 'riggs' are turned abreast

Another season has commenced
With uncanny speed
After the soil preparation
Comes the sowing of the seed!

CHAPTER 6

MECHANISATION ON THE FARM

With the introduction of the first tractors, namely the 'Fordson', which was a rather small and basic machine, the heavy working horses were phased out, and this signalled the beginning of major changes on the farm.

None of the existent farm implements were suitable for attaching to a tractor, so it was here that the local village blacksmiths came into their own.

For a time, the number of horses that the smith would get to shoe, dropped dramatically, until many years later, when it became fashionable for parents to buy their children a pony. These were more or less kept as pets then, as Riding Schools with Instructors and things like Gymkanas, were unheard of until many years later.

As horse riding became more popular, the price of

horses and ponies went up, so the mares were often bred without much thought, or regard, to bloodlines or confirmation, with the result that the countryside became awash with often rather inferior quality foals.

When they were put on the market, they often proved difficult to sell, so were sent to Auction Marts, where quite a few were sold to Butchers, probably ending up sold again for human consumption on the Continent. Thankfully, I think less of that practice goes on nowadays.

I remember when I was about ten, asking my dad for a Shetland pony, but I got an emphatic; "NO, who is going to feed it and groom it before you go to school in the mornings?" That was it, I went quickly off the idea, as I was never a morning person, not even yet.

From shoeing heavy horses, the Blacksmiths soon became very busy removing shafts from horse drawn implements like carts, harrows, binders, mowers and rakes etc, before replacing the shafts with tow-bars.

Some implements however, could not be adapted, like ploughs for example. These had to be bought new, and in those days there wasn't much in the way of spare cash to launch out with, so the change-over, of necessity, was a gradual process. It was always a source of great interest to near neighbours, if some new-fangled implement was bought, they were always brightly painted in greens, reds and blues, I don't recollect yellows being used.

Once the horse carts were fitted with tow-bars, it was found that they were economically too small, so the four wheeled lorries were tried out. They were unsuitable for some purposes, as they didn't have built up sides, so a new type of cart was marketed, which tilted. These were, of course, fitted with inflatable rubber tyres, unlike the original horse carts, which had large, spoked metal wheels.

They were a great advancement, and useful for carting turnips, fertilisers or dung, from the cattle courts to the fields in the summer, after the cattle were put out to grass.

A fairly important new innovation, was the convertion of the mower and binder to suit the tractor, as the binder was a very hard pull for sometimes, two and even three horses, especially if the fields were hilly or sloping. This uneven land could also be dangerous for tractors, if the grain was cut down hill, the tractor usually went up the hill empty, that is, not cutting, which is safer.

Across the slopes of a steep hill can also be tricky, as the machinery can slide and in extreme cases, may flip over, which can result in thc driver being trapped, or even killed. For this reason, men should never work alone on dangerous hillsides, it was much safer with horses, as they are sure-footed, though the task was very hard on them.

Sometime later, perhaps into the late fifties, the

Combine Harvester was invented. This was a great boon for the farmer, as they not only cut corn, barley or wheat, but also I think, oil seed rape. The Combine, as the name would imply, also acted as a threshing mill, so both tasks were completed in one operation. It was of course desirable that the crop was cut when dry if possible, as the grain had to be stored, and if not dry, it would 'heat', or mould, and go into growth.

To make sure that the grain was dry enough for storage at the end of the operation, a grain dryer was invented and erected at lots of the bigger farms. The smaller farmers had to transport the grain to commercial dryers in order to make sure that moisture content was dried down to 15%. At that percentage, it would then be dry enough to store in barns for the winter, until it was required for malting, if the quality was very good, or for feeding if it didn't quite make the grade.

The arrival of the Combine more or less put an end to the travelling Threshing Mill, pulled originally by a Traction Steam Engine. These monsters would arrive early in the morning, around 6am, as it took some time to set the mill up in the correct place between two rows of ricks, so that two rows could be threshed together without moving the mill.

To be operational, the travelling mills as they were called, required approximately fourteen workers for all the tasks involved. The extra hands were lent by neighbouring farmers for the day, or days, whatever was necessary. All the farmers would help each other in the same way until the threshing was complete.

Threshing with a steam mill was a dusty, tiring job, the final task being the carrying of sacks of grain or barley, weighing between one and a half and two hundred weight, upstairs to a loft, usually on the back of a hefty worker.

No wonder the older farm hands were often bent and crippled with Arthritis, for as well as the carrying of such heavy weights, they were out in all weathers, so often worked long periods whilst soaking wet, that was of course, before the days of oilskins.

Another implement which covered a great area at one go, was the manure distributor, and drill sowing machine, which combined sowing seeds and fertilisers in one operation. Things had moved on in leaps and bounds from the days of the Hopper, or

‘Happer’ as it was locally known. It was a sort of oval shaped, canvas bath, which the worker strapped to his front by means of a harness. Grain was placed in the happer, then the operator filled his hands alternately with the seed, first the right, then the left and scattered it in a semi-circular motion as he walked forward. It was a very rhythmic sight and soothing to watch. The grain grew up evenly instead of in parallel rows, as it does with modern machinery.

Following the drill sowing machines, the sprayers were a more recent invention, with the advent of enough chemicals to kill everything under the sun, from mildew to creepy-crawlies, but hopefully not the humans who eat the grain in the form of bread, etc, at the end of the process!

The tractor ploughs were made of strong iron, as they frequently hit stones, some quite large, and were prone to damage. To begin with, they were single furrow, as was the horse ploughs before them, but as the tractors became bigger and more powerful, they became capable of ploughing up to eight or more furrows at a time. They were designed to ‘set’ in furrows from above and below, and were what is called reversible, which makes turning at the ends of the drills quicker, and in their own space.

One of these ploughs pulled by a powerful tractor can plough a large field in a single day, whereas a man with a pair of horses and a single furrow plough, would clock up miles in that one field, plus he would have had the added difficulty of walking in a narrow straight line on the bottom of the furrow!

When it came to haymaking, the hay was cut and left to dry in the sun, it was gathered up in rows using a wooden rake-like implement approximately ten feet wide, with the teeth lying flat on the ground. This was pulled forward by a single horse until the rake was full of hay, the load was then upturned, in a sort of head over heels fashion. This implement was called a 'Tumbling-Tams' and the teenage boys were frequently given this job, which they seemed to enjoy.

The next procedure was performed by a metal rake on wheels. This rake had a seat on it and the teeth were placed fairly close together, and were curved so they could roll up the hay. The heaps of hay were then built into small ricks or 'Colls', as they were called, before being dragged by a chain, which went around the bottom of the coll, to a central place, usually at the top of the field, and once there, built into full sized ricks.

Because the hay was thoroughly dry, it would keep well. If at all damp, the ricks would 'heat', and then had to be turned over and rebuilt. Hay was, and still is a very valuable crop for the animals in winter, but haymaking involved a lot of work and was dependant on good weather, hence the saying; "Make hay while the sun shines."

The tractor version of the tumbling-tams was called a

'Sweep', the wooden teeth were much longer and were tipped with pointed steel or iron for durability. The sweep was attached to the front of the tractor and pushed forward until it was full of hay, then the load was released by simply reversing the tractor, leaving it to be built into ricks.

About the time of the hay sweep becoming the 'in' implement, a new theory became known, that hay could be cut and stored before it became dry like hay. This would defeat adverse weather conditions. The idea was to dig out a pit and concrete the sides like walls, then fill the pit with finely chopped moist grass or hay.

This was then packed or almost 'trodden' with the heavy tractor, which impacted the heavy mass, forcing out a lot of the air and causing the grass to ferment, forming silage.

Liquid drained out of these pits like a dark syrup as a result, and oh, it did smell. This residue proved a problem if it reached ditches and eventually the rivers, as it caused pollution in the form of algae on the surface of the river estuaries.

Quite a few years later, balers were used to pick up and bale both the hay, and the silage, then about a decade ago, these bales, which were large and round, were rolled in black plastic to keep them weather-proofed. This was a great advancement, as they could be stored along the tops of fields if inside accommodation was not available.

There was one difficulty with these bales and that was their weight. It was then necessary to invent a machine with spikes on the front, to dig into the bales and hoist them up into either a 'bogie' or lorry, or to pile them high for storage. This implement was called a Fork-lift or 'Buck' rake.

The digger also came into being about then, which put an end to manual digging of large areas and was used to dig out the silage pit, drains and foundations etc. The job tackled depended on the bucket attachment used, which was attached to either the front or rear of the digger. This implement was classed as a specialist tool and was often owned by a Contractor, who did the work on hire, as it was not economically viable for farmers to buy this expensive equipment when it was not required on a regular basis on the farm.

A long corkscrew like tube called an 'Auger', was to replace the manual carrying of grain up to lofts in sacks, and was used for loading grain in and out of grain dryers and stores.

All this modern technology meant a big change was taking place on the farm. The number of men required to run a farm was drastically reduced, so the workers gravitated to work in the towns in factories and later, drifted into the construction and oil industries. Farm workers were usually hefty lads and good workers, so found alternative employment fairly easily. Often the workers lived in 'Tied' cottages so had to move house when they gained new jobs. These houses were later either rented or sold to people moving into the North-East, now prosperous with the advent of the oil exploration, as well as the Gas plant and Hydro Electric station, all of which required hundreds of workers in the construction stages.

These events brought many changes to rural areas, not least to the local schools, where English voices became as familiar as the local Doric. Supermarkets sprang up on the outskirts of the towns and cities, and subsequently the livelihood of the village shops, not to mention the mobile shops which had served the countryside so well for so many years, were practically brought to an end.

The local Post Office had helped to keep the one village grocer alive, but not for much longer, as families were well-off by now and most owned a car, so went to Supermarkets once a week to stock up at prices the country shops could not possibly match. The country bus service was also reduced, or in some cases, stopped altogether, for the same reason.

CHAPTER 7

OUR RATHER EARLY 'ALL-MOD-CONS'

Looking back to the thirties, we were well in advance of some of our neighbours, with regards to 'Mod-Cons'. When the house was built in 1929, provision was made for hot and cold running water, and also electricity. My dad was responsible for providing this electricity by means of a rather noisy powerful engine which was bolted to a substantial cement base for stability.

I didn't understand the workings of that engine, except for the fact that there were several belts and pulleys involved. The machine was situated in the garage so that it was near to the house for convenience. Under the same roof, there was a storage unit with two or perhaps three rows of hefty shelves made of strong mahogany timbers, which held rows of oblong shaped glass containers, called Storage Batteries.

They were filled with lead slides and covered in acid, which was stored in large bottle shaped, vessels which had a straw or raffia basket-like protective covering. They were shaped like the bottle gardens of today, only the acid ones were marked with lime-like scales inside.

There was approximately sixty of the glass storage containers, and somehow, when the engine was not thundering on, they stored electricity. From this storage, we could draw on enough electricity to provide light for the house and steading. I never remember the menfolk using hand lamps in the steading, so presume that we never required them.

The engine did need to be switched on and running for jobs like washing, which was done by a washing machine bought at the Glasgow Exhibition of 1938. It was a 'Beattie', a Canadian make, which suited our voltage of 110 volts, unlike the later grid voltage of 220.

It stood fairly high on four castors and was round in shape, with an automatic wringer that swivelled from the tub to the sink, or whatever. It was painted in a soft green colour, while the interior was a very good quality aluminium. The Beattie was sold just after 1950, by which time we were linked to, what was known as 'The Grampian', being the source of electricity at that time.

Some years later, we bought this washing machine back from the people we sold it to, as by then, it had been adapted to 220 volts. Why we re-acquired it, I don't know, perhaps we both trusted and admired it, the machine certainly served us well, twice.

We also needed the engine running when the ironing was being done, which task normally lasted for hours, as at the time we had nine people living in the household, including my invalid grandmother.

In those days, unlike to-day, everybody had a 'Washing Day', when the bulk of the washing was done. This was certainly true of the 'average household', when everybody started off on a Monday morning with clean clothes, which had to suffice until the following Monday morning.

People living in towns had a specific day and time to do the washing and had to share a communal wash-house and drying green, and if they were lucky, a loft. It would never have done if every household had pleased themselves when they chose to do the weekly chores, it would have ended in civil war!

At that time of course, boilers had to be lit. There were no dryers to pop the soaking wet clothes in if their day happened to pour with rain. Only the fire in the kitchen/living room was available, upon which usually, all the cooking was done as well.

Can you imagine present-day wives putting up with steaming clothes draped over anything and everything, including overhead pulleys. Not much wonder houses had condensation and that the occupants suffered from chest complaints, we do have it much easier nowadays.

An added task for country families, often living without running water, was to arm themselves with buckets on Sundays, (religion permitting), and carry water in preparation for washing the clothes, (perhaps out in the open), on the next day.

On our farm we were lucky enough to have running water, which we obtained by means of a windmill. From my earliest recollection's the windmill was there, standing bolt upright, making a statement.

I presume it had been constructed when the house was built in 1929 and was part of the plumbing system, as it was used to pump the water for the house and the steading. This was taken from a well in the middle of a field some distance away, to a collecting cistern, some then went to the steading and some to a tank in the loft of the house.

It was constructed of galvanised angle iron and was supported by four legs, roughly six feet apart, which formed a square reinforced by a band of metal about three feet from the ground. The legs tapered up to a platform, perhaps two foot square, which would have been about twelve foot from the ground.

Upon this platform, was erected a large wheel, with foot wide 'slats', to catch the wind. The wheel was about eight foot across and made the whole structure appear top heavy. There was also a central column, which disappeared into the ground and was attached to the pipes that ran all the way to the well.

There was a slim metal ladder attached from the ground to the platform as the wheel had to be adjusted according to the wind direction. Because of its height, the windmill was frequently damaged in bad weather, or high winds. Although my heart used to be in my mouth watching him, my dad used to think nothing of climbing to the top of the windmill, to do running repairs.

During the war, I can clearly remember my dad often climbing up to the platform to look out to sea and the surrounding countryside to see if convoys were being attacked, or where bombs were being dropped inland.

There was one occasion which springs to my mind, when dad was on his look-out post and a German raid was in progress. An airman from the local airfield was with us that day and when a German aeroplane approached the farm, machine guns blazing, he began to shout at my dad to come down.

Though there were now tracer bullets flying in all directions and everyone, including the airman, were petrified and running for cover, my dad stayed right where he was and appeared totally unconcerned by the event when he finally came down from his lofty perch.

After many years, the windmill became redundant, when it was replaced by a pump. It was then dismantled when it began to disintegrate as it became dangerous. The water pump, latterly an electric one, had a distinct disadvantage in winter, in that if it was not properly covered and protected, it froze. It then had to be thawed out with boiling kettles, which could prove to be difficult if the water supply had run out before the frozen pump had been noticed! If the conditions were severe enough, there was a power failure and therefore no electricity to boil what water we had.

Many people today possibly have never seen a windmill in action and certainly, thinking back, there weren't many windmills around even during the war, but they were certainly functional and effective.

Myself and Miss Murray
with the Windmill in the background

CHAPTER 8

CHILDHOOD SUMMER PICNICS

Looking back on special occasions which I will never forget readily, these included Sunday summer picnics. Somehow, the weather always seemed to be dry, warm and sunny. When you were a child, I suppose that couldn't always have been true, but children never seem to remember rainy days, only the 'special' days.

The picnics I had in mind, were a visit to see the King and Queen with their family, attending Crathie Church for Sunday worship in August, while on holiday at Balmoral. I can't remember going every year, but certainly we went several times before the war, that is, up to 1939.

My father had the use of my Grandmothers Austin 12 saloon car for these occasions, in children's eyes, quite a magnificent ride. The bodywork was maroon, with black trims, mudguards, wheels etc, and a fair bit of glistening chrome. I remember the number plate quite clearly; AV 2333. Needless to say, I can't remember the number of my present car, without going to the garage to look!

The Austin had a mahogany dash board, complete with a round-faced clock, which you had to click open and expose the back, in order to wind it up. The clock was removed at some time, I don't know why and was around the house for years after.

The upholstery was maroon leather, finished in a sort of padded style, which was in lined sections, very like the seats in the House of Commons for example. The carpeting was also maroon. Outside the car, the 'running boards' were wooden, covered with ribbed rubber, to prevent your feet slipping. I think the headlights protruded from the front of the car. The body looked square and box-like, which gave plenty of head, leg and arm room, a necessity, as it seated a lot of people.

Sometimes stools were put behind the front seats for the 'small people' to sit on, leaving the ordinary seats for the numerous adults. The boot folded down from the back where the picnic crockery and pans of food were stored in a wooden box and securely strapped to the back.

Food was generally a large roasted fowl, a pan of scraped potatoes and tins of peas. I think the sweet was something in the nature of a fairly solid and stable trifle, with the cream separate, perhaps an apple or date tart was also included.

We also carried a Primus stove, a kettle, pans etc and went to a quiet spot and set up a fire sheltered from the wind, otherwise the Primus didn't burn properly. It was always my dad who was in charge of the stove.

Travelling rugs were taken to sit on and a tablecloth

was laid over one, where plates and cutlery were set out. All in all, it was quite a grand affair, sometimes we even had a guest join us, a local hill shepherd. We had to be very careful to look out for ant hills when setting out our rugs, it could prove to be quite painful it you happened to sit on one!

The Royal family went to Crathie Church around 11am - 11.30am and the service lasted one hour. Hundreds of people lined the steep hill up to the Church from the main Deeside road and when the Royal cars appeared, the crowd began to cheer and wave, the children often waving flags. If you arrived early enough, you got a place at the front, which commanded a good view.

This outing was certainly the highlight of the Summer holidays and meant a lot to tell your schoolmates about, after the return to school at the end of August.

On the way home from Deeside, we stopped along the route to boil a kettle for tea and whatever, returning home in the early evening, happy, often tired and usually sunburnt. We always brought home a bunch of heather, usually sticking a small bit onto the radiator cap which was on the front of the car bonnet.

One other favourite spot for a Sunday summer picnic, was the village of Collieston. I think it is one of the most beautiful coastal villages that I have ever seen. It always gives me the impression that it could well be on the Continent, or, if it was surrounded by trees, perhaps Devon, neither of which places I have seen in reality, but on the television often.

We set off in the fore-noon, having prepared most of the food the night before, arriving in time for a quick swim before the thought of the mid-day meal even crossed our minds. The car was parked well down on the sheltered concrete pier, well up to the sun, all day. The concrete drew the heat and by mid-day, felt quite hot on our bare feet.

My dad and myself were the swimmers in our family and we spent the day going in and out of the warm water. Dad used to dive in off the pier, but that was a bit on the high side for me, as at that time, I was only ten, at the most, so I just waded in from the sandy beach.

The area, even then, was full of young families out to enjoy a good day out, and that's exactly what they did. There was the odd little paddle boat, with the adults keeping a close eye on any young budding sailors! On the beach, the children with pails and spades were at the ready for a bit of sand-castle building before the tide came in again.

On various small areas of ground, posts were erected and nets suspended in squares. On these nets, the small fishing boats dried the catch of whiting, after they were gutted and split. They were dried flat and then became 'Speldings'. These were freely available for sale to visitors and when you went home, these speldings were cooked on a flat, hake-like metal contraption, in front of an open fire. This gadget was called a 'Brander'. When cooked, the fish were slim and quite hard. You ate them with your fingers, either tearing them open, or lifting off bits. They were quite different to anything else I had tasted and were delicious.

At the end of a long and happy day, it was a case of pack up and head for home, ascending the steep brae out of the harbour area in first gear, in order to reach the road at the top in one piece.

Once home, the car had to be emptied, the sand laden, damp bathing costumes and towels, shaken well outside before they were taken into the house to await the washing day next morning. That left the dirty dishes and pans to be washed, by now looking disgusting as the food was well dried in. Once washed until gleaming, these were then put away into the cupboards again.

There was seldom any left-over food, as any bits and pieces had usually been given to the seagulls, always anxiously hovering overhead, or the odd friendly dog belonging to other visitors, sitting close by. The stove was emptied of paraffin or methylated spirits, whichever one it took. Sometimes we took the odd stool or folding chair, but more often or not, we had cushions and travelling rugs to sit on.

After everything was cleared away, there was nothing

left to do but have a good wash, put Calamine lotion on to hot, burning necks, shoulders and arms before enjoying a cool drink.

Tired, but content, we then wended our way to bed, the picnic over for another year, but it's memories remained, to linger on for many, many years.

Collieston was a wonderful place where time seemed to stand still, with no-body being in a hurry, and where every action was always performed leisurely.

CHAPTER 9

MY CHILDHOOD WAS ABOUT TO CHANGE

When I was a few months passed seven years old, something started to happen to me that I was to learn later, would have a devastating effect on my entire life. I was too young to understand what actually was taking place in secret locations away from everybody. I was being sexually abused and didn't realise it.

This carried on for over four years, despite being referred to the family doctor twice. He was an elderly, severe looking gentleman who unfortunately didn't have a 'way' with children. Nothing was ever done to put a stop to this practice, so whether he gave his opinion on what was taking place, I shall never know.

At the same time, my mother, with whom I had never developed a bond and showed no real affection for me, often blamed me for the problems she had to cope with healthwise. She would say; "I have never been well since you were born," as though I had asked to be born. The more often this was said with meaning, the more hurtful it became.

I was also frequently kept from school under the pretence that I had to help. I was quite aware that I was becoming isolated at school and was lacking in confidence. I couldn't tell anybody what was happening to me for several reasons, firstly, I didn't understand myself, and as time went on, I thought the abuse was something that happened in every family.

I didn't know that it wasn't supposed to happen and that it was quite wrong and illegal. I wouldn't even have understood what illegal meant. It never entered my head to tell anybody, and anyhow, I would have been too shy and possibly embarrassed to do so.

Realistically, where would I have got any information which would have led me to believe that something was radically wrong? Sixty years ago, there was no television, only radio. We more or less only listened to the news and programmes like 'Tommy Handley', The Goons and music like 'Grand Hotel'. The only magazine that was bought regularly was the 'Peoples Friend'.

Bodily functions were never mentioned in our household and there was no sex education in schools in those days. Even married women tried to hide the fact that they were pregnant. The only information that reached our ears, was that babies were found under gooseberry bushes. Rather an uncomfortable and prickly bed the poor mites were supposed to have had!

Finally, a last, but very big reason - just who would have believed me, if I <u>had</u> <u>known</u> what was happening and been able to tell. It was very likely I would have been accused of telling lies and not believed. On reading books now, that's exactly what seemingly did happen.

I saw on the television recently, a family of four sisters, all of whom had been abused by the same person. Not one of the sisters told, or knew that the others were in the same position. They are adults now and fifteen to twenty years later, the perpetrator was taken to court and is serving a prison sentence.

CHAPTER 10

SUMMER SWIMMING TRIPS

I was only really happy during that time, if I was in the company of my father, whom I adored. I remember helping him to plant cabbages which came in bundles of one hundred, from Lothian. where they were grown, to the nearest railway station. They were mainly Savoys', a hard, green, curly cabbage which withstood the winter, so providing greens well into spring.

I also did a little bit of carrot weeding, but that was tedious to me, too tedious, as it took a long time for me to see any progress that was made. The carrots were grown quite near the beach, which during the fine days of summer, I visited almost on a daily basis. I was always accompanied by several of the farm workers children, of which there would have been about eight at the time I am writing about.

Armed with bathing costumes, sometimes towels, a bottle of lemonade or dry, fizzy powder which was mixed with water to make a sweet lemon, or orange drink, off we went. Usually we also had a packet of 'Hard' biscuits, which were common to all households in those days.

We knew the beach like the back of our hands and preferred when the tide was just beginning to go out, and leaving a narrow strip of water up to three feet deep. There were of course no waves to scare us as they were out to sea at this point. The water was lovely and warm, as before the tide came in, the sand that would end up under the strip of water had been warmed up by the sun. It was like our own private swimming pool.

We would have been in and out of the water till it drained away, or sank into the sand, by which time it was homeward bound for tea. Tired but happy, and sunburned into the bargain. My tan used to last well into the winter, complete with crosses on my feet under the straps of my Clarks sandals.

CHAPTER 11

WARTIME

When the second World War broke out in 1939, what followed fairly soon, was that huge, square blocks of concrete were placed in three rows deep, brickwork fashion, in the areas of dips in the sand dunes, where the various burns entered the sea.

There was also three rows of coils of barbed wire, strengthened by steel pipes in a sort of scaffolding. These stretched along the coast and were meant to deter tanks etc from landing on the beach and venturing inland, in the event of an invasion from the enemy.

Surrounding the dips in the sand dunes, around the cement blocks, the Royal Engineers laid three rows of land mines. Unfortunately, during the war, several of these mines were set off accidentally. Wandering dogs were sometimes responsible for setting off a land mine, as they entered the mine field in pursuit of a rabbit, the rabbit being too light to trigger an explosion.

One Sunday afternoon, I clearly remember a terrible tragedy occurring. This afternoon was always a popular time for adults and children to take a walk over the bents, or sand dunes and the beach. On this particular Sunday, a pleasant day in the autumn, two boys, about twelve years old, were on such a walk.

For some reason, perhaps they followed their dog, they went through the barbed wire and entered a minefield. One mine went off and I think, killed one boy and seriously injured the second.

The police and army were quickly informed, perhaps by my father, or a wartime coastguard station near the rocks, I don't know, maybe we had the nearest telephone. A doctor from town and also our shepherd, arrived quickly on the scene. There was a difference of opinion as to the exact location of the mines, as the strong winds had blown sand over the area and hid any trace of wires etc.

The army thought they knew their way into the minefield and a corporal went to disconnect the area, so that the boys could be taken out and the life of the injured boy saved if possible. Things went tragically wrong, as the corporal stepped on a second mine, which exploded, killing him instantly, along with the second boy.

The doctor and the shepherd received shrapnel wounds and had to be taken initially to a First Aid station, then later transferred to Aberdeen. But as they were actually military casualties, they were soon transferred to Stracathro Hospital, which was some considerable distance for relatives to visit their injured.

I seem to have heard my parents say, that neither were fully fit again, our shepherd had scars on his forehead and suffered severe headaches. He moved house and his old house was empty for several years.

After the war was over, the mines were removed, but no guarantee could be given that they were all gone, as the spring winds had blown layers of sand over the minefield. After a few years, we became fool-hardy and went through the area to gain access to the beach. The concrete blocks were not dug out, but disappeared and re-appeared depending on currents and the wind. The now rusty barbed wire was also removed and life in the area returned to near normal.

While we couldn't go to the beach, we had changed our swimming venue to the river. Being fresh water, the water currents were a little more difficult than we were used to, but it was a lovely feeling sitting on a big stone or rock and letting the river water flow over your feet.

Wading was a little more difficult as the bed of the river was covered with stones, though with the constant motion of the water, most were rounded. This all happened before the up-river villages and towns emptied sewage into the rivers, and the water authorities withdrew water for reservoirs. Though our beach and river expeditions were not supervised by an adult, we never came to any harm.

By the river, there were sheep pens, which were used by the shepherd to retain the sheep and lambs, while he removed them singly, to; of all things; wash their bottoms and tails!! If the sheep had worms, which they got from grazing on contaminated grass, they tended to get rather messy. At that time, worm drenches were not available, or invented. The only measures that the farmers could take, was not to over-stock and keep rotating the grazing.

In 1938, my grandmother on my father's side, came to live with us, as she had had a severe stroke. She was totally helpless and had someone looking after her during the day, who also lived with us. In the evenings, another lady came from the town by bus and cared for her during the night, returning home in the morning, again by bus. This made for a busy household.

When war was declared a year later, we were advised to protect our windows with sticking strips of cellophane type of paper, usually blue coloured, on the inside of the glass in X and O's fashion. If there was a bomb, the glass would then stay in large pieces instead of shattering and injuring anyone within the room.

In my granny's room, there was also wooden frames with netting wire stapled to them. This was for double security, as my granny could not be taken to our safe place, under the stairs.

If there was an air raid, the siren blew, but we were also telephoned because my dad was an air raid warden. This telephone warning was given because he had to be on the look-out for fires, as if that should happen, it would have attracted bombers. The war would have been underway for approximately nine months by then.

We also had frames made for most of the downstairs windows, but this time, black felt was attached, and all were fixed to the windows by brackets fitted with thumb screws. That way, no light escaped, which was a crime punishable by a fine. A special shield contraption was also fitted onto the headlamps of the few cars and buses that were on the road, to reflect downwards what little light we were allowed.

Shop doors were fitted with box-like shutters and hung with what was known as blackout curtains, to save any light escaping when the shop doors were opened. There were of course, no street lights.

Everybody carried a torch, but batteries were sort of rationed, so were always very scarce. Cinema's did function, but if there was an air raid, it was flashed up on the screen and you could leave then if you wished. Sometimes there were air battles over towns. You knew they were uncomfortably near and should run for cover if you could hear machine gun fire, or at night, could see the lines of tracer bullets.

I remember, my aunt was staying with us once when a raid was on, so we all crowded under the stairs and my mother had bought a supply of tea cosy pads, one each, and we were instructed to put these on our heads, we must have looked really stupid. There were no steel helmets for civilians. It must have been a real scary night, as my mother's dentures started to chatter. My aunt said to her; "For the love of God, take out your teeth."

Raids took place any time day or night, sometimes more than one in the course of the night. One Sunday, from one of the upstairs windows, we saw the result of one such raid - three craters were visible and quite a number of sheep were killed. Bombs also landed on the rocks at the edge of the sea and shook our house, causing our ceilings to crack sometime later.

The main school was hit twice and pupils were thereafter taught certain subjects elsewhere, in other suitable premises, like church halls. This meant a fair bit of walking between classes for children, an excuse for loitering certainly, but also, which was not so pleasant, to get wet frequently.

Two days before war was declared, my dad was at the local market and as a reserve RAF man, he was called up for service and had to leave that night. By then, he was aged 44 and a little on the old side. He spent five months in the RAF, going between Montrose and Evanton in Rosshire. He was able to spend a short time at home at weekends to see to the farm.

I was ten when my dad left and, to compensate for his absence, he organised that a local cabinet maker, who stocked baby and dolls prams, should send a dolls pram out to me on the bus and I was told to go down to the end of our road to collect a parcel.

I duly stopped the bus and asked the male conductor if there was a parcel for me. The conductor said; "A parcel," with a note of surprise. He then went to the back of the bus lifted the door of the boot and lifted out a wrapped up dolls pram with a smile on his face.

The wheels were not tied up so I was able to push it up the road quite easily. It was tan coloured, shaped like a Carriage hung pram, only there were no springs. It had a collapsible hood and a rain apron. I was extremely proud of my new pram, which I later gathered, cost 29/-, old money.

The only pram I had had previously, was an apple box, painted with pink paint, even over the Mackintosh Red labels. This was what was called blackout paint, used for painting electric bulbs.

A blue colour of the same paint was used on skylights to prevent lights being seen from the air. The paint never really dried properly.

The local blacksmith attached two pairs of wheels, which along with the box, I carried to the Smithy. He also put on an iron handle. I think he took pity on me, as there was really nothing attractive about it. But it served my purpose, that is, until the arrival of my grand new pram.

During the war, the nation was encouraged to grow more food, especially grain and vegetables, as bringing in food by sea was becoming increasingly more dangerous. Submarines, aircraft and warships regularly attacked food convoys, sometimes sinking the Merchant ships, resulting in a great loss of seamen's lives.

Everyone with a farm, a plot, or even a garden was encouraged to 'Dig For Victory'. Farmers were ordered to cultivate grasslands and plant more barley, or wheat if the climate was suitable, also more potatoes and vegetables.

With the outbreak of World War II, some of the younger farm hands were called up for service in the Armed Forces and, after a year or two, farm labour needed to be augmented by prisoners of war, or civilians, in the form of displaced persons.

Locally, these men were mainly Italian, though I recollect a few Poles, and also the odd German. They were brought by truck from the Prisoner of War Camps first thing in the morning and collected around 5pm, or, before dark if it was winter time.

The prisoners were accompanied by a guard, or guards, depending on how many men were in the work team. They were fed on the farm, with rations obtained with coupons provided by the Ministry of Food. Like our own food during the war, their diet was pretty basic, a good substantial soup with bread, and a steam or milk pudding. Sometimes corned beef, mashed turnips and potatoes were available and, perhaps a 'Mealie Dumpling'. Meat however, was always in short supply, as was fruit.

Very little fresh fruit was seen in Britain during the war, so if a supply did come to town, the news spread like wildfire and queues quickly formed at the shops. We were allowed one pound of fruit per ration book, while stocks lasted.

That brings me to ration books. They were small buff coloured booklet type things with pages for separate commodities like tea, sugar, butter, marg, fat, jam, bacon, meat, bread and flour. You were allowed a number of ounces in most things per month. Sugar was 8ozs per week, tea - 2ozs, marg from 2-4ozs, whilst butter varied and the jam ration was 1lb per month. The meat ration was 1 shilling's worth, plus 2 pennies worth of corned beef.

Sweets were also rationed and the monthly allowance was usually 12ozs. I don't know what children of today would think of that, but they probably wouldn't have the problems they do with so many tooth fillings if sweets were still on ration!

Coupons were also necessary for clothing and I think something like sixty to seventy two were available per year. I do remember a few examples, shoes were seven per pair, stockings three per pair, a dress was seven. Coats and suits were rather greedy on the allowance, perhaps twelve to fifteen. Wool was also bought with coupons.

Newly weds got vouchers for things like blankets and sheets, I can't remember about towels. People used to wash and boil flour bags for tea towels, while aprons, dresses and summer blouses were sometimes made from curtain materials which were coupon free.

Speaking of curtain material, reminds me of a dear, old lady, called Miss Reid, who had done sewing for the family for years. She was very crippled, with what had probably been arthritis, and I recall she walked with two walking sticks. She also had breathing problems and had to sleep sitting propped up in bed, with about half a dozen pillows.

She had a very small house, consisting of; a bed sitting room with an open coal fire, a small kitchenette, and another small room which was usually full of customers sewing material. In her living room/bedroom, she had a single bed, several chairs, one of which was an easy chair sat by the welcoming fire, and a substantial chest of drawers, quite high, if I remember rightly, on which stood a rather nice antique clock which chimed.

Last, but certainly not least, a large old fashioned treadle sewing machine, which was boxed in around her to shield her from draughts from the door, as she had lots of callers. There was however, no table, so how she managed to cut out the material around the sewing patterns, I shall never know. From the curtain material, she made two summer dresses for me, with knickers to match. One had a white background with smallish red flowers throughout, the other was a pale green with sprigs of flowers all over it. Both had puffed sleeves, which were a bit of a nuisance to iron.

I would have been about twelve at that time, and when I outgrew them, they were handed down to someone less fortunate. Miss Reid also made school blouses from what was perhaps, curtain lining, which she also made into aprons, bound with pale blue bias binding. Come to think of it, I never saw her with a pattern, she was so clever perhaps she didn't need one, there aren't many like her around to-day.

Next door to her house, there was a large Draper's shop, which sold every kind of material you could wish for and my mother had asked Miss Reid to make two pairs of pyjamas each for the family, including my dad. The material was duly chosen, it was pale blue, with creamy fawn half inch wide stripes.

Miss Reid collected the whole roll of material rather than leave the shop to cut off 'X' number of yards, that way, she saved material. Being an extremely economical cutter you never got huge pieces of cuttings, for repairs. When she had the amount she required, she returned the remainder to the shop, measured what was left, then deducted the length of the piece she had cut off, my mother then paid the shop. When ready for bed and all dressed in our new stripy pyjamas, we must have looked like a pack of escaped prisoners.

Also during the war, this same drapers shop made a dressing gown for me, out of grey army blankets. It was trimmed with green felt, also coupon free. During the making of this extremely warm garment, the machinists broke five sewing machine needles, so I don't think they agreed to repeat the offer to anyone else!

Furniture at that time was made of rather basic designs and generally of flimsy construction. Again, the newly weds had priority for the essential items. I am not sure whether other members of the public were free to purchase items of furniture, carpets and rugs, which I gather were rather scarce.

Linoleum was generally thin and of poor quality, but a better quality was sometimes available for naval boats, generally dark brown. Occasionally, quantities of this found it's way into private homes. All wartime goods, especially clothes and furniture, was specially marked with a sort of logo which was called a utility mark.

In the summer of 1940, the evacuation of Dunkirk

took place, after the German Army pushed the British Army back over the English Channel. For those who remember that occasion, it was truly a miracle of the twentieth century. There were many casualties, but most were rescued, in boats of all shapes and sizes.

The returning Highland Division troops occupied a field in a nearby picturesque hamlet, surrounded by trees, which provided good camouflage for the many 'Bell' tents, which were coloured green and khaki.

Being sited near the river, I presume it provided the men with washing facilities, being June and therefore relatively warm. This hamlet had never seen such activity buzzing around, and hasn't since. I can't remember how long they were stationed there, hopefully, until they had had a good rest after their dreadful ordeal.

Our steading was also used for accommodation for troops, I think they were 'Seaforth Highlanders', which was part of the Highland Division. The Captain and the Lieutenant shared what was normally my bedroom, but the family had all moved downstairs because of the bombing. The troops occupied the barn and loft for sleeping accommodation and the cart shed became the Cook house.

The cooking stoves were mobile and were probably fuelled with oil or gas of some sort. They used lanterns which they were anything but careful with in their use. My dad had to warn them repeatedly about exposing naked lights, as they could be seen from the sea.

Trenches were dug in our garden in three different places, and as far as I can remember, were only used for manoeuvres by the troops. We were never sure when there was going to be a mock battle.

I remember, one soldier spent twenty four hours detention in what used to be a wash-house, with a built-in brick wash boiler and an old incubator big enough for hatching a hundred eggs into chickens. The shed had a red tiled roof and a concrete floor. There was only one small window about nine inches square, with the glass missing and as the door was padlocked from outside, there was no chance of escape.

There was nothing for the soldier to sleep on and not even a wooden box to sit on. Late at night when it was getting dark, my dad was dispatched with sandwiches and a mug of hot cocoa in case the poor lad had not been fed. This he handed in through the glass-less window. I believe the soldier's crime was that he had scampered off to town when he was supposed to be confined to barracks, or more appropriately in this case, our steading!

In August, 1940, my grandmother died, it was a Wednesday evening. The funeral, I think, took place on the Saturday morning from the church where, when she was younger and in good health, she was a regular attender.

She was very respected in the community and was the only grandparent I ever knew. Though she was a semi-invalid before her major stroke and unable to be an active granny to me, I respected her and loved her very much. She used to give me half a crown for my Christmas and birthday presents. That money was always put into the Savings Bank.

I was not at the funeral, but sent to a neighbour, where I spent the day. I was in the habit of taking their baby out in the pram, which was quite safe as the roads in those days were practically free of traffic, because petrol was rationed and therefore in short supply. I don't think that children attended funerals in those days anyway, so I was unable to accompany a very gracious lady on her last journey.

A few months after the outbreak of the war, everybody was issued with gas masks, in case the Germans planned to use gas on the people of Britain, which thankfully they never did. But nevertheless, we had to be prepared. Every member of the Armed Forces, the police, civil defence and all others who were not strictly speaking, civilians, were issued with rather elaborate gas masks, housed in a flattish, khaki canvas holdall affair, which was slung around their necks and rested on their chests.

From time to time, they had to have practice sessions at speed, where they had to perform their normal duties wearing these fearsome black contraptions with rubber tubes coming out of them.

The civilian equivalent was much less elaborate and fitted neatly into a squarish, cardboard box. Most people bought a canvas cover which fastened by the means of two press-studs, it had a long strap which went over the head and one shoulder and the box hung about waist height by your side.

We were duty bound to carry our gas masks everywhere we went and my dad had to go around the local district at regular intervals to inspect the masks to make sure they fitted accurately.

When they were being worn, everybody looked 'Pig-headed', complete with black, round snout and grey rubber straps framing a sort of windscreen. This very quickly steamed up, with the result that you couldn't see where you were going. I believe that babies had some sort of apparatus that they were entirely tucked into and which must have scared the living daylights out of the poor little mites.

After the summer holidays in 1940, I went to live with an Aunt and Uncle who lived near a village inland, going to school there for the winter term. My cousin was more or less the same age as me and in the same class. There was also another boy and girl who were from the town school and had been moved out because of the bombing. This was because the air raids then were fairly frequent and quite a bit of bomb damage was done. I came home at the weekends and returned in time for school on Monday morning. I enjoyed my time at that school, which I went to by bicycle from the farm.

I learned to milk cows while I was with my Aunt and Uncle, my cousin and I would race each other home on our bicycles, change into our old, or play clothes, before dashing to the byre, to help milk one or more cows each. Why we were in such a desperate hurry, was because the race 'winner' got the chance of the cow with the biggest teats, being naturally easier to milk, as we had more to hold on to!

One I remember stood at the farthest end of the byre, she was black and white, as most of them were, being either Friesian or Ayrshires, I can't remember rightly. There was roughly twelve or fourteen altogether, but she was my No. 1 target, as she possessed lovely big teats! All the cows were very patient with us junior milkers, we would only have been ten or eleven years old at the time. Strangely, I don't remember us ever volunteering to help with the 6am milking, I wonder why!

After the cows had all been hand milked, the milk was cooled and bottled, before my Uncle delivered it to the local village using a Shetland pony and a two wheeled lorry. This he did twice a day, fresh milk was fresh in those days! It was a great thrill to me when I was allowed to go with my Uncle on the lorry and deliver bottles of milk to the doorsteps.

People like my Uncle, who worked with dairy cows cleaning them out then milking them, seemed to acquire a peculiar odour, that hung around them and invaded even the house. I don't know if it was splashed milk or 'pre-milk' fluid, which permeated into their clothes, and which they never removed when coming into the house. With wellies and overalls, I suppose things are different these days. After the Christmas holidays, I said goodbye to the Friesian's and Ayrshire's at which time, I returned to the town school.

Upon my first day back, I was asked to inform the school where my parents had arranged for me to run to in the event of an air raid. A sister of the lady who was my granny's night nurse, lived practically next door to the school and kindly said I could go there.

It was a very substantial granite house which used to be the old 'Jail'. It had spiral stone stairs down to the basement and several children sheltered in one of the cells. There were no windows and the cell was about nine feet long, by five feet wide and had seats along both sides.

There was something, perhaps a small table, holding a small candle, which by the time we arrived, was always lit. This dear lady always gave us a biscuit or a sweetie, which in wartime, couldn't have been easy. Being underground, you didn't hear anything, so I presume someone must have kept an ear open for the 'All Clear' which meant the risk of bombs was over for that particular time.

Sometimes, when I was cycling home from school, which I did when the weather was fine, the siren would go off and that was a bit scary. I remember one morning, around 9am, when the children were walking up the hill to a nearby village school, a German plane appeared and opened fire with its machine guns at anything that moved. None of the children were hit or injured, but quite nearby a horse was killed and in the opposite direction, the reins of a horse ploughing in a field were cut. on this occasion, the handler and the horse escaped without injury.

Further along the coast, some school children hurriedly abandoned their bicycles and crouched in a ditch, they too escaped injury, but were naturally very frightened. The plane flew very low, which gave little warning as it wasn't heard advancing towards you.

The North-East of Scotland was the nearest point to Norway, where the raiders came from. Often their targets were convoys of shipping, heading South with cargoes of food from across the Atlantic. If a ship was unlucky enough to be hit and sunk, when there was a high tide, or strong Easterly winds, debris of various kinds would be washed up on the beach.

Often there was large quantities of wood and big, hefty deck hatches with metal handles which could be used to make a bridge over a ditch etc. Parachutes were also found, these had been intended to be used to drop ammunition to the troops. I think these were confiscated by the customs.

One memorable time, a fairly large quantity of MacKintosh apples washed up and people arrived like flies in a great scramble. Men were opening the boxes and stuffing the apples down their trouser legs, which they had first tied at the ankles of course. With trousers bulging at the seams, it would have been a rather uncomfortable walk home for them!

Prams, home made 'hurlies', bicycles, and really, anything that moved, was utilised to carry the prized apples. There was even talk of a hired lorry being used, which was said by the men involved, to be from the Custom and Excise, but I don't think this statement was ever proved, one way or the other. We had some, and I have never tasted such delicious apples before, or since. There is something to be said about the joys of forbidden fruit!

As well as apples, sugar and flour were washed in, but I rather think they were ruined by the sea water. Containers of lard also occasionally appeared and I can remember my mother buying a zinc dust bin and melting down the lard on the top of the stove in the kitchen. This was distributed to friends to augment the fat ration, which allowed a little more baking and possibly a few chips, to be cooked in neighbouring kitchens.

CHAPTER 12

LOCAL DEFENCES

Quite soon after the outbreak of the war, it was considered necessary to build facilities for air defences, in the form of an aerodrome for fighter squadrons so that planes would be available quickly to attack the German bomber squadrons.

A large area of flat ground was, I presume, bought and work progressed at speed. Runways and taxiing areas were built of concrete, hangers were constructed and roofed with corrugated iron. Underground shelters were dug and covered with earth over reinforced structures for air personnel. Several of these are still visible fifty years on.

Separate from the airfield, were the billets of the servicemen, and in other places, there was a hospital, a canteen and most importantly, an operations room. This was built underground and was a very secretive place as far as the neighbouring civilians were concerned. 'Hush, hush', was the expression used.

All the outside of the buildings were painted in heavy camouflage, which was hoped to make the building inconspicuous from the air. The aircraft were also painted in the camouflage colours of green, brown and khaki, but with the RAF logo clearly visible, in order that other crews could easily recognise friend or foe, so preventing a 'friendly' attack.

There were quite a lot of casualties amongst air crews, mainly pilots, as the planes were Spitfires and Hurricanes, which were singly manned. Bomber crews, on the other hand, may include two pilots, as well as a navigator, bomber and gunner(s), who manned the guns for self defence.

There were various nationalities stationed at the airfield. As well as British airmen, there were Canadians, Polish and Australians, each playing a big part. The multi-national aspect was again brought to my notice recently, when I paid a visit to the Cemetery, where no less than nineteen of those airmen killed in action are buried.

They are lying at rest along the back wall of the cemetery, each with a grey headstone, all very similar, with their number, rank and the name and country of the unit they were attached to.

Of the nineteen graves, approximately half were British, one was Polish, one Australian and the remainder were all Canadian. The average age would have been about twenty two or twenty three, but what saddened me in particular, was a Pilot Officer in the Canadian Air Force, who was a mere nineteen. A laddie who hadn't started to live, his life stolen away from him.

I heard that their relatives had been over to the Cemetery to see the graves and were so impressed with the way they were being looked after, made a cash donation. This was used for a lovely, long wooden seat, which is placed near to the graves, for the use of visitors. A lovely gesture of appreciation.

I had thought that there were graves of German pilots but I could not find them. There were German aircraft shot down locally but perhaps it was over the sea.

There was another airfield built along the coast, further north, but I don't know much about it, except that it was situated between two coastal villages and was a Fleet Air Arm Base. It was under the command of the Royal Naval Forces who wore navy blue. With little civilian movement on roads in those days, because of petrol rationing, I saw little of the bases to the north, or their personnel.

With the Army based in the town and Motor Torpedo boats in the port, the Cinemas, restaurants and the NAAFI, were kept very busy providing food and entertainment for the uniformed men and women in their off-duty time. Queuing for the Cinemas was very common then, especially at weekends.

Towards the end of the war, Miss Murray, the dear lady who had looked after me when I was a toddler, was hit by an army truck whilst crossing the street during a snow storm. She was badly bruised about the body and had received injuries to her head. She was looked after by her friendly neighbours, in her own warm, feather box bed, which few people still possessed. She was in bed for a week or two, but didn't seem to fully recover.

Her nephew and his wife eventually persuaded her to go to Glasgow to live with them as she was at the stage where she was unable to look after herself, especially as she lived in a small flat on the third floor.

In those days, there weren't the homes for the elderly that there are at present, so she really didn't have an option. She was very comfortable and well cared for, but I believe her heart was still in her home town. Miss Murray never returned, but after she died in 1951, she was brought back to be buried.

She had always been a very regular church goer, so it was rather disappointing and sad, that the Minister forgot about her funeral at the cemetery and someone had to go and fetch him.

CHAPTER 13

SIGNS OF REAL EMOTIONAL PROBLEMS

I moved up to the Academy at Easter, three months before my 12th birthday but, as I was always rather heftily built, I was larger than most of my class mates. After the summer holidays, we were joined by lots of country pupils from the outlying villages. We were then placed in the various grades of classes, depending on our capabilities and wishes.

The cleverest pupils were entered for languages, the next grade was French and Commercial, which was where I landed, and the third grade was called Technical. The commercial subjects consisted of French, Shorthand and book-keeping. The other subjects were the usual; English, Maths, Science, History and Geography. We also got domestic subjects, such as cooking and sewing. Last, but certainly not least, was Art, the only subject throughout the entire years of my education, in which I ever achieved a 'First'.

I was not particularly bright, but this was understandable, as I was frequently absent. When my mother had spells in bed, I had often to stay at home and help and I hated every minute of it! The more I had to help in the house, the more I hated it and it made me feel very moody, withdrawn and miserable.

This came to a head one day when I became so

withdrawn, that I crouched in a corner and refused to speak to anybody. I didn't understand until 1996, that what was happening to me, was partly due to my mothers attitude toward me and also a reaction to the sexual abuse I had experienced earlier in my childhood.

My mother had always blamed me for her health problems, which incidentally, were imaginary part of the time, this, plus the emotional effects of the abuse, left me so unhappy and insecure.

I was not a spoilt child, though my behaviour may have been interpreted as such, in fact, I was the odd one out, as my two brothers were the loved ones, as far as my mother was concerned. My dad attempted to humour my mother and at the same time, comfort me, but he didn't see what went on when he was outside working.

I had a real problem, but no-body realised the fact, let alone understood. On that awful day, when I was so miserable, the family doctor was called. That helped!! as by that time I was so afraid of him. He and my mother suggested that I be <u>sent</u> to a boarding school, but thankfully, my dad put his foot down.

By the time I was three months short of fourteen, I had only attended school two days in three months. Those two days were only as a result of being seen by one of my teachers while out for a run on my bicycle one evening. I was supposed to go back to school after the summer holidays, but by then I was much bigger than my new classmates would have been, so I flatly refused.

My emotional problems continued, because I was still at home, doing what I still hated. I wouldn't get up in the mornings, and, at sixteen, I was taken to a Psychiatrist. He was a gentleman of around forty-five, other than that, I can't recollect much of anything else. He spoke to me and all I remember, was that I was supposed to wash my face and arms with COLD water to wake me up! I had two further appointments with him alone, and that was supposed to be my problems solved!

A few months later, I was sent to the School of Domestic Science, what for you may ask? To learn to cook, sew and how to 'Clean a House'.

At least I enjoyed the sewing, and have done so ever since and the company of other girls was a pleasant change for me. We usually had a half day on a Wednesday when a few of us would go to see a film.

I was in digs with a very pleasant elderly lady who was an excellent cook and despite rationing, produced lovely meals. The 'Course' I was on lasted six months and then I returned home, where it was back to square one.

CHAPTER 14

WORLD PEACE AT LAST

It was a great relief to everybody, when peace was declared, and the hope of life returning to normal. After nearly six years of hostilities and fighting in many countries in Europe, Africa and Asia, many nations were left with tremendous problems facing them. In some countries, bomb damage left cities, towns and villages in ruins, and the lives of the people concerned shattered.

There was scarcely a family in the British Isles, who if they didn't lose a member of their own family, knew someone who had given their life for peace. Victory celebrations for those who had lost loved ones, may have been impossible, but all over the country, people engaged in street parties, fireworks displays and lit bonfires, while Church bells again rang out in joy, after being silent for so many years.

The streets were lit again after being in darkness for what seemed like forever and blackout curtains were made redundant. Everything didn't happen overnight, but at least the powers that be, could start again to plan for the future.

The men and women who were in the Armed Forces were not demobilised for some time after and when their turn came, were issued with civilian clothing, generally referred to as the 'demob' suit. The clothing generally, was rather basic and of a somewhat inferior quality, but at least it was a welcome change from uniform dress.

Rationing continued for some years after the end of the war, as factories and warehouses had to be converted or rebuilt to cope with peace-time requirements. Food had to be imported and shipping was of course badly hit, as many ships had been sunk.

It must have been very difficult knowing where to start, in order for the wheels of peace to start turning again. Item by item, rationing was discontinued, but I remember that clothing coupons were still in use in 1949, and perhaps a year or so afterwards. Tea and sugar was still on ration in 1952, while sweet rationing continued until 1953.

The summer following the end of the war in 1946, it was suggested that I should accompany an older cousin, who was going to stay for a few weeks with her sister in London. We were to travel south by over-night train and sleepers were booked, in those days, there were four sleepers per compartment. A husband and wife were allocated the other two, we hadn't expected a gentleman to be sharing our sleeping quarters, which would mean that we couldn't remove our skirts. The next morning, as you may anticipate, we looked decidedly crushed and dishevelled.

We had something to eat with us and also a flask of

tea. On the previous evening, my cousin and the other couple had produced pills from their respective handbags or whatever, and proceeded to wash them down with the tea, I did not understand until later, why they were all taking pills.

It was then into the bunks and heads down, I was on the top bunk, with the gentleman opposite. We had passed Edinburgh, and were heading for the borders, when I became aware of the contented snores of my fellow passengers, hence the pills! I observed every station all the way to London without shutting an eye. My travelling companions woke up as bright as buttons, while I felt like a dead dog!

We got a taxi from the station, to the home of our host, who suggested a bath would freshen us up, I certainly needed it, if for nothing else to keep me awake. After that we had a lovely breakfast and the sun was shining in more ways than one.

My cousin took me sight-seeing and also got me used to the bus routes, and of course, the underground. Once I was familiar with the means of travelling around, I was released on my own into the big City.

I was in my element, whether shopping, or just window shopping. I remember I went into Selfridges, where I found turquoise nylon taffeta in the material department, which I bought enough of for an evening dress, along with a paper pattern. I also bought a piece of dark salmon pink material to make an evening skirt with, I was delighted with my purchases as that type of material hadn't reached the shops in the North yet, nylon being a fairly new fabric.

Another day, we went to Kew Gardens, which I enjoyed, as already I had quite a keen interest in gardening. Later the same week, I set off on my own, to search out the 'Norland School of Nannies', and when I found it, I stood outside the grounds and just looked at it for a very long time. From a young age, I had always said that I wanted to be a children's nanny, but the idea was knocked on the head by my mother, who said that it was far too lonely a life.

There was no arguing on the subject, the answer was a firm NO. Nannies certainly came in a category between 'Upstairs' and 'Downstairs', I suppose you could say, somewhere on the 'Landing', so it probably could be a lonely occupation. That didn't stop me wanting to do it, which was why I stood so long, dreaming of what might have been.

After two enjoyable weeks in London, I travelled home by train alone, accompanied only by my purchases. At least I had returned with something exciting and interesting with which to occupy my attention, in the shape of the material I had bought to make my evening dress and skirt.

Later on in the year, when the nights became too dark for outside jobs in the garden, I thought it was time to start on my dress-making. We had an old treadle sewing machine, with wrought iron sides, making it very heavy to move, which was too bad, as I had to pull, push and lift it, from a small room where it was stored, into the warmth of the kitchen every time I used it.

I had to spread the material out on a large table and place the paper pattern on top of it, this was then pinned to the material before I cut out the various shapes. I then pinned the appropriate pieces together before sewing them with large hand stitches. I didn't have a dressmakers dummy which made fitting myself rather difficult, but with a little experimentation, the end product turned out remarkably well.

After my success with the dress, I decided to attend Evening Classes to see if I could improve upon my rather inadequate education. I attended Maths and Commercial English, which I thoroughly enjoyed. The English especially, I felt helped me considerably, as it was quite different from what little conventional English I had learned at school. It was interesting, which made learning easier.

I remember our teacher stood at the back of the class, and repeated in a dramatic tone of voice; "Variety is the spice of life, it is also the spice of good English!" As I was deficient in great chunks of my education, you will not perhaps be reading good English here, but I hope I have succeeded in giving you a bit of 'Spice', through the relating of the 'Variety' in my life. The following winter, I decided to make a dress from the other material brought back from London. This time, I had to use a different textured material and dye it the same colour as the skirt for the bodice, before joining them together, as I had decided to make a matching top!

I trimmed the bottom of the skirt and the end of the sleeves of the top with black velvet, which I felt produced a good contrast of colour and an attractive finish. I was more than pleased with all my learning efforts so far!

When I was nineteen, I decided to have another go at learning to play the piano. At seven, I had been told I had to take music lessons, but at that age, I wasn't interested, however I was sent and that was it. I never hit it off with my music teacher and had to be ordered to practice. The music I was given as practice pieces were tuneless and meant nothing to me, they had titles like; 'The Merry Miller' which I had never heard before and was unlikely to ever want to hear again!

This went on for several years with me progressing absolutely no-where, I sometimes played truant, with the daughter of the Chief Constable, no less. When my mother discovered my truancy, the arrangements for my lessons was changed, the music teacher coming to my house to give me my lesson.

She then had tea, after which I had to escort her to the bus, all of which was worse to me than the first arrangement. Eventually, my music lessons thankfully came to an end, but by then I was beginning to acquire a taste for the popular Classics, hence my renewed interest when I was nineteen.

As a pupil at the Academy, I had joined the school orchestra, made up of all violin players. We were issued with glorified, oblong plywood boxes complete with strings and that was our violins! Later, I was able to borrow a violin from a relative, but I had a real problem, in that I was short-sighted, so I couldn't see where my fingers where landing on the strings, the resulting effect was frequently a peculiar squeak, which was decidedly out of tune.

However, my earlier efforts notwithstanding, I approached the Head Music Teacher at the Academy and, as a result, began to attend weekly lessons at the house of my school music teacher, and made fairly reasonable progress, with pieces by Schubert and Schuman beginning to trip from my fingers.

After my lesson, my teacher always played me a short piece by my favourite composer, Chopin, which gave me a pleasant send-off for the bus home. Fortunately, or unfortunately, depending if you asked me or my teacher, my lessons came to an abrupt end, when I was accepted for nursing training at Aberdeen Royal Infirmary.

PART 2

TO THE PRESENT DAY

CHAPTER 15

THE HAPPIER YEARS

After four and a half years at home, feeling dis-satisfied and unhappy most of the time, I finally managed to get away when I successfully applied for a vacancy to start a nursing career at Aberdeen Royal Infirmary.

I got a date for the interview and arrived there to discover there were also four other girls waiting to be interviewed. We waited our turn in silence, all were a bit apprehensive, this was a big day.

When my turn came, I was shown into a room, where, seated behind a large, flat topped desk, sat Matron. My first impression of her was that she resembled Queen Victoria. She was short, stockily built and was dressed in a navy blue dress, with a little white lace collar round her neck. On her head she wore a white starched cap, trimmed with narrow lace. She wore glasses, and when she spoke, her voice was somewhat high pitched with a suggestion of a tremble.

After the interview we were given some sort of test involving designs of green triangles etc, and had to spot the difference. We seemed to have pages of these to do in a short time. Some time later, I received notification that I had passed, and was given a date to start early February 1949. I can't remember if the other girls interviewed the same time as me ended up in the same intake, or later.

We were given a list of things to bring with us and included in this list was three pairs of stockings. There was little to choose from at that time as to the type of stockings, pure silk being too expensive and almost unobtainable, so that left 'Lisle', which was a sort of cotton. These stockings came in two varieties, first quality, which was called 'Fully Fashioned' and second quality.

The fully fashioned stockings had shaped feet and a shaped seam up the centre back of the leg. When wearing them, great care was taken to make sure that the seams were straight as it was considered slovenly if the seams were twisted or rucked. These stockings tended to be more generously made, as far as width and length of leg was concerned, which proved a great advantage, if like me, your legs tended to be rather overly covered with what is generally termed as FAT.

By the time your stockings were attached back and front, and sometimes at the outer sides as well, to rather tight suspenders, this area of fat tended to get bunched up. After walking up and down a busy ward from 7am to 6pm, the area could become rather reddish and tender, as though on fire.

The other cheaper stockings were seamless, with little or no shape in the feet and the legs were straight as compared to the shaped fully fashioned ones. The tops were also tighter and of less expanding material. They were almost impossible for the heftier of us poor mortals to wear. When you bought a pair of these seamless stockings and discovered your mistake, you certainly didn't repeat it!

Though the war had been over for nearly four years, many commodities were still rationed, including clothes which could only still be bought with clothing coupons. These were like stamps which were cut out of small books as each purchase was made. I remember that each pair of stockings required three coupons, so that was nine to begin with!

Another item on our list of things we had to provide for ourselves, was a pair of black shoes. With durability in mind, rather than comfort, I chose strong black lacing shoes with crepe soles. I soon discovered I had made a big mistake with the crepe soles, as the hospital had underfloor heating. With all the walking around we had to do each day, by the end of a busy shift, our poor feet were on fire. The feet of the lisle stockings nearly stood up unaided by this time, especially in hot weather, as they were sandwiched between boiling hot feet and my thick black shoes complete with even thicker crepe soles!

The stockings were duly washed out in the hand basin at night, often with toilet soap in an effort to sweeten them up a bit! We then draped them over a string under the hand basin, where they would be dry by morning. The next day, they were so hard, you would have thought we'd washed them in starch, so we rubbed them vigorously between our hands in an effort to make them soft enough to be wearable.

When the time came for them to be darned, which was usually sooner, rather than later, the six-stranded black thread was split into three strands, in an attempt to make the resulting darn look slightly less bulky. The thinner thread also helped to prevent a blister occurring, which by the end of the day had you walking in a one, two, three, hop, sort of fashion.

All this was endured in the name of 'Caring for the Sick', - which Sick? My feet were killing me! The junior nurses seemed to get all the running about to do, it was certainly 'In at the deep end.'

When nylon stockings became available, the shops used to keep a pair, sort of under the counter for regular good customers, these were only worn on special occasions and treated almost with kid gloves. The shop assistants used to open up the pack and carefully slip a well manicured, slender hand into the leg of the nylon stocking, to show you how sheer they were, as this 'thinness' was something entirely new.

If by chance, you happened to snag one of your precious stockings, you took it back to the shop, where it was sent away somewhere, to have the ladder repaired at a charge of 6d, or 2.5p per ladder. This gave the stockings an extended life span.

At this time, I had an Aunt in Canada, and she used to enclose a single, washed nylon stocking in a letter to me, the second would follow in a later letter. If both had been sent together and unwashed, the receiver would have been charged Customs! We tend to think that the age of Red Tape began in the present day, not true, as our Custom avoidance exercise proves!

As nylon stockings became a little easier to obtain, I used to buy mine in Esslemont and MacIntosh, who stocked a make called, 'Taylor Woods'. These were almost as beautiful and as comfortable as silk. Though they cost a little more and my monthly salary was only in the region of approximately £7, I thought the stockings were worth the sacrifice.

To return to my arrival into nursing, we were instructed to report to the Nurses Home by 6pm on the date given in our acceptance letter. We were shown to our rooms in alphabetical order and my room was next to the Sister Tutor's room, so I had to be careful to keep the noise down at all times.

The rooms were all very much alike, gloss painted walls, which I seem to remember being a pale, creamy yellow. Each room had a built in wardrobe with a deep shelf on top and there was a three drawer chest alongside it with a mirror built into it. We had a bed, bedside cabinet, small wooden chairs and a small rug, there was also a wash hand basin.

We were instructed to assemble in the front hall, so we could be escorted to the dining hall in the main hospital, in time for supper at 7.45pm. The dining hall was a long building with a very high ceiling. Up both sides of the room were at least twelve tables, each seating eight people, with a wide passage up the centre. The senior nurses sat at the front of the hall, and as we were the new recruits, we were shown to the very last three tables, which gave the existing staff plenty time to have a look at what a motley lot we were!

In those post-war years, there was no choice of meals, we either ate what we were given or did without. We were each presented with a plate on which sat pieces of Cod roe, I however, had never eaten this in my life before and certainly wasn't going to start on that particular night. Unfortunately, my 'dietary preferences' meant that I went without, so ending up very hungry!

On the top of the table were plonked two teapots with hinged lids. We didn't know then, that when they were empty, we were supposed to flick open the lids, and the maids would come and replace them, consequently, some of us didn't even have a cup of tea. Here endith our first lesson!!!

After supper, we all went back to our rooms, where we unpacked and got acquainted. We then visited one another, introduced ourselves and chatted about various things. After a while, we dispersed to our new homes, to get ready for bed in time for our curfew; which was lights out at 12 midnight. The following morning, a maid rapped smartly on our bedroom doors at 7am - it was time to get up and face a new day, and a new life.

The first week was spent being shown around and being measured for our uniforms, which were made up in the sewing room. As the material was not pre-shrunk, they were made far too big and miles too long, they did however, improve very slightly with time!

We also were medically examined, and X-rayed etc, then, to round off the week, we were immunised against several diseases. At 5pm on Saturday, we departed for home until Sunday night, what we did not anticipate however, was that we would be 'nursing' very painful arms as a result of the injections, so woe betide anyone who bumped into us!

During the next eleven weeks, we had lectures from the Sister Tutor on Anatomy, Physiology, Hygiene and Diabetes. We were also taught the correct way to make beds for various occasions like; Admissions, Theatre cases etc.

I recall one Saturday at teatime, around 3.30-4pm, I went up to my room to prepare for going home after dismissal between 4.45-5pm. I put on my skirt and jumper under my uniform with the idea I could save time, as I was catching a bus home at 5.30pm from Mealmarket Street. Usually, it was a mad rush, from Schoolhill past the side of Marsichal College, in order to catch this particular bus, hence my 'disguise' brainwave!

As fate would have it, this Saturday I was chosen to be the patient for a demonstration of changing the sheets with the 'patient in bed'. Probably I was chosen because I was the bulkiest nurse there out of our crowd of twenty four! Not a great honour as it turned out, especially as my skirt was made of thick Harris Tweed. I certainly never succeeded to save time that day, or indeed in that manner again!

For some reason which I found difficult to understand, we were all taken on several tours of inspection. Our first being during the initial few weeks of our training, when we went to the Municipal Waste Disposal Works, near the harbour! In a huge warehouse, the lorry loads of household rubbish were tipped onto a long conveyor belt, elevator type structure.

On either side of this moving belt, there were lots of

women dressed in dirty overalls, with caps on their heads. On one side, the women picked out all the glass bottles and jars etc, whilst on the other side, the tins were removed for recycling and I think everything else was incinerated.

The air in the building was full of dust, I don't know what those women earned, but they were certainly worth every penny!

Later, we were taken to the Rowett Institute, but I can remember nothing of that visit, except that the heel came off one of the girls shoes, resulting in her hopping and limping between the various buses until we got back to the hospital.

Our last visit was to Kingseat Mental Hospital at Newmachar. I thought the grounds there were lovely and restful. I remember thinking it sad, that everywhere we went, the doors were locked and the staff carried bunches of keys. I was very impressed with the Occupational Therapy unit, and thought that the Therapist had a very worthwhile job, that of bringing a little joy into the lives of the less fortunate of us.

At the end of our first twelve weeks, we had to sit exams on the various subjects we had studied. These first weeks were called Preliminary Training School. We were now ready for the real world, and there was great interest in the notice board, where our names and the Wards we were destined for, were posted up.

I was heading for a male Surgical Ward, where the Sister had quite a reputation for being a hard task master. Everyone was a bit on the slow side to begin with and tended to 'fumble' their way around, but on this ward, you had to learn mighty quickly, or you were in trouble. Tidying up of the utility room, or 'Sluice', had to be done before 9.30am, when the junior nurse went for breakfast.

Invariably, after everything was spick and span, an older nurse would come in and dump an armful of dirty linen, or worse, and then depart. At that point, Sister would appear, "Why is all this linen lying about, this should have been cleared up by 9.30!!"

You couldn't win, and you dare not say anything, no, no, not in those days!! Discipline was very much part of our training, with everyone being addressed by their proper title, even your closest friend were addressed as 'Nurse'.

I spent three months in the surgical ward, from May to the end of July and my poor feet felt every minute of it, as the junior nurse walked up and down the long ward, many, many times in the course of a day.

Often, on Admission days, extra emergency beds were put up along the middle of the main ward, and on such occasions, it was possible to have forty patients for a day or so. Next day, a few patients would be sent home and the extra beds would then be dismantled, and reasonably normal services would be resumed.

It was usually the junior's job to answer the telephone and you had to be careful to give the correct response to the correct enquirer who was wanting to know how their sick relative was, before finding the Sister.

My three months were now up in my first ward and provided I got a satisfactory report from the Ward Sister, I was due to move on. All being well in that regards, I was moved to the Gynaecological Ward, where naturally all the patients were female!

There, all the wards were smaller, which was fine for privacy on the patients side, but meant a lot more running around for we nurses. There were also more short-stay patients and some day patients, which meant they were to-ing and fro-ing to Theatre, almost on a daily basis.

With all the resulting bed changing, the amount of linen we went through was tremendous, thank goodness I wasn't responsible for the laundering! Even checking the clean linen upon its return from the laundry, was a huge task on a daily basis. The linen was counted, then checked, before being sent to the sewing room for repair, if necessary.

Again after three months, I was moved, but this time, I was destined for my first Night Duty. For some reason, we had to work till 12 noon, before moving to sleeping accommodation in Aberdeen, in either a corner house on Queen's Road, or a similar but smaller house in Great Western Road. This meant moving all our belongings, and vacating our original room, it amazed me how much I had collected in a few short months! A van transported our luggage, but I can't remember what our mode of transport was.

After we had settled in, we were then supposed to go to bed, to prepare for our first nights work. We were awakened around 8pm, then we were taken to work in a double-decker bus. I always seemed to land on night duty in the depth of winter and will never forget, nights in mid December, going through the residential areas on the bus and admiring all the lit up Christmas trees in the windows. It was like Fairyland. As we descended from the bus, we were a sight to behold, all fresh clean uniforms and wide awake looking. I suppose there must have been about sixty of us, plus the Night Sisters.

During the night, we had our meals in reverse, which took a little getting used to. We started at 8.45pm, before going on duty, with tea, bread, marg and jam. Around mid-night to 1am, depending on which sitting we were sent to, we had lunch, followed by tea and buns at around 4am. We finished our night shift at 8am, when we went to breakfast, then travelled by bus back to our sleeping accommodation.

I was sent to a female Medical Ward, these could often be very busy, with blood drips to keep an eye on, for patients with Haemorrhages etc. Medical wards were considerably smaller than the Surgical Wards, and tended in those days to have more long-stay patients.

They were often elderly ladies, who had had severe strokes, were often paralysed and had lost, or partly lost, their speech. Life was very sad and dull for them and every long day must have seemed the same, washed, hair done, bed made very early, followed by a cup of tea at 6am, then sitting through the same daily routine until bed time.

On night duty, we worked six nights on and two nights off, and it seemed that week in, week out, the same ladies were still there. Nowadays, these patients would be moved onto a Residential or Nursing Home to make way for acute cases.

Illnesses seem to have changed with the new advances in medicine and medication and some problems are seldom heard of today. I found this medical ward rather depressing and was quite pleased when my three months was up, which meant we were all off on two weeks holiday.

It was now February and the nights were starting to get lighter. When on night duty in mid winter, there is little opportunity to spend any time in day light, when you have to sleep during the day. After a time, this can affect your health, so the two weeks holiday helped to restore our health and also, re-charge human batteries.

Back from holiday, into yet another room and ready for a few weeks in the classroom again. This time, the subjects of the lectures were more specialised and mainly given by the Consultants, who had a habit of dictating much faster than it was possible to write. Afterwards, it was a case of; "Did anybody get that bit?" "What bit?" "The bit that came after *so and so* and before *such and such.*"

The new subjects were; Surgery, Medical, Gynaecology, Ear Nose and Throat, Skin and Eyes, quite a variety. There was a lot to learn before what was called the 'House Exams'. Especially for me, as I had to leave school at fourteen years old, while most of the other girls had come into nursing straight from school. I wasn't the possessor of a good memory either so that didn't help, but somehow or other, I did manage to pass all my exams.

After the exams, we were sent to the various wards, we hadn't been to before, so that we gained experience of all departments. Theatre experience was also included, which was a bit hair-raising to begin with. The Surgeons could be rather short tempered and would zoom in on a new face, which tended to make you all fingers and thumbs!

Any noise, like equipment falling on the floor, was a disaster, as surgical bowls or dishes were either made of enamel or stainless steel, so when they fell on a marbled-like concrete floor, they made a tremendous noise. I wouldn't dare repeat the resulting comments from the Surgeon, even the look from the Theatre Sister was enough to have you shaking in your shoes.

The atmosphere was always tense, which was understandable as human beings lives were at stake. Whilst doing our shift, there was lots of cleaning to be done, tiled walls were washed down every morning and again at the end of the day. All equipment was washed and cleaned with methylated spirits, while each instrument had to be cleaned, counted and boiled. Swabs were counted before and after each operation so that all could be accounted for, before a wound was stitched up.

Before a nurse finished her stint in Theatre, she had to assist the Surgeon with at least one operation, usually an Appendectomy or a Hernia. I wore glasses, which tended to steam up, so had difficulty seeing properly to thread needles with nylon or catgut for sutures. Nervous, shaking hands didn't help much either, especially with Surgeon's not famed for patience!

I had a second session in a smaller, more homely operating theatre, which was mainly used for Dental or Facial surgery. Sometimes it did get used for injuries and there were also cases of Facial Cancer, which could be quite upsetting.

The Cancer Surgeon was around fifty, and quite a character, with a great sense of humour. On occasion, you were tidying up between operations, preparing for the next patient, before you realised that he was making fun of you.

The theatre was only the size of an average sitting room and everything required for the operations had to be fitted in there. The operating table was sat in the middle of the floor, all around it were instrument trolleys, an anaesthetic machine, sterilisers, sinks, one or two surgeons, the nurses, an anaesthetist and of course, the patient. You could say, we were rather crowded!

One one particular occasion, I was scrubbing instruments in the sink, with great gusto I may add, in order to get them into the steriliser as quickly as possible, when suddenly, everyone looked in my direction and started to roar with laughter.

Apparently, the surgeon had been studying my scrubbing technique, before remarking; "She'd make a great set at scrubbing a 'Sark', or shirt." My face immediately went on fire, whereupon more laughter erupted. He was a very human and popular man.

My last night duty was spent in a ward for non-emergency surgical patients and I loved my time there. The patients were seldom seriously ill, mainly male, and always in good spirits. In a small ward, a farmer had as his companion, a magician, who had been performing at a Theatre in Aberdeen.

They seemed to spend all day writing notes to me on toilet rolls, one word per page. The pair of them were insomniacs and insisted on getting a cup of tea, whatever the hour, as long as the Night Sister wasn't due for her rounds!

While on this night duty, the yearly hospital dance became due and even though you were on duty, someone could stand in for you until midnight. This was all arranged and another nurse and I, along with our partners, were ready at 8pm for a good evening.

Matron and the Senior Sisters were there to keep an eye on the proceedings, so it was a case of soft drinks only. However, things seemed to be a bit stale, so we decided to go down to the Caledonian Hotel for a 'quick one'. We downed them rather quickly, but seemed to be alright and as there was a buffet of some kind, the food also appeared to have helped.

There was a large crowd and the proceedings warmed up a bit, then before I knew it, it was 11.45pm and time for us to leave. The night was frosty and when I hit the fresh air, after the warm atmosphere of the dance hall, my head started to spin, and 'What-ho'! I felt like Cinderella, having to return before mid-night. I was attired in a beautiful white broderie anglaise evening dress, but by the stroke of 12, with a little help, I was transformed back into 'The night nurse'.

The night sister wasn't due to pay a visit until her 2am round, so after several cups of strong coffee, I passed the test and nothing was said, although the patients had a good laugh, they were great sports.

About the time of my last night duty, there were strong whisperings going around the hospital, that the little dog belonging to a Senior member of staff, had digestive problems, or, in plain language, suffered from Constipation.

Occasionally, the Enema tray would disappear from the Sluice room of a nearby ward, to be returned in the same secretive manner, some time later on the same night. This was outwith the normal time that any Enema's would expected to be administered to the human species!

Surely a dietary change and a bit more exercise would have been a simpler way to treat the problem, it certainly would have been more comfortable for the canine in question, and a lot less messy!

Following that spell of night duty, we were all back in the classroom again, to study for our final exams, all depended on these exam results. It was a very tense time for all of us as the time approached, but we felt we could only do our best. The written exams were spread over several days, then we had to face the orals and practicals, which were more hair-raising.

After a few weeks, the results were posted up on the Notice Board. It was a mad rush to see who had passed and who unfortunately had failed. Only two or three had to face the disappointment of failing, the rest, including myself, were fortunate enough to have passed.

Some weeks before we were given our results, we had all made enquiries about our future plans. A few of the girls decided to stay on at the Infirmary as Staff Nurses, while the majority chose to take further training, mainly Maternity.

I, along with a friend, chose to take our Maternity training at the Simpson Memorial Maternity Hospital in Edinburgh, while others went down the road to Aberdeen Maternity Hospital, the remainder choosing to go to Glasgow.

I had sick leave to make up, having had my tonsils out, and later injuring my back, so I left at the end of June 1952. My friend and I were not due to start at Edinburgh until the 1st September so that would give me a fine break.

Before we all went our separate ways, we did what every group did, we went out and celebrated the same evening after we had completed all our final exams in the afternoon. This ended a very nerve wracking ten days, so naturally, we were all very jolly. We had our photographs taken in groups and also some of the entire class.

According to the photo's, the venue appears to be in an attic, but where, none of us can remember! The photo showed us standing, with a piano in the background and the ceiling appeared to be sloping. I have no reason to believe that we were anything other than reasonably sober, so it is disappointing that no-one can remember where we actually were at that point! However, I guess we must have all had a whale of a time!

I can imagine we probably spent a large chunk of our salary that night, which amounted to the princely sum of just over £9 per month by the end of our training. We had to stay in the Nurses Home until we were qualified, unlike it is nowadays.

Students had to be in then by 10.30pm otherwise the door was locked, we were only allowed one late pass per week until 11pm. Occasionally, for the more adventurous, the ground floor windows proved a handy way to gain access on those occasions when a late pass was not forthcoming!

Before we received our salary, which we had to queue up for on the last day of the month, certain deductions were made, namely our board and lodgings, laundry, tax and national insurance. We were left with £6.15/- per month during the first year, which was increased in the second year, when we ended up with just over £9 at the end of three years.

The nurses who stayed on as Staff Nurses, got £15, but those of us who decided to take further training, went back to receiving £9. I remember after a further years Maternity training, my pay was £32, but that was living out.

I shared a top floor flat at the top of Holburn Junction, which was furnished and cost £10 monthly. It required quite a bit of energy to climb up the eighty four steps from ground level, plus twelve steps down to the coal cellar, as we had a coal fire.

I was on night duty for quite a lot of the time I lived there, and sleeping during the day was rather difficult as the Tramcars were still in operation then and they stopped just below our windows. Also there was the problem of the newspaper salesmen shouting out the latest headlines. That all seems a long time ago now.

During July and August, 1952, I went home to keep house, while my mother had an operation and convalesced. At the same time, I made some preparations for my departure to Edinburgh in September.

Now we were free to buy clothes without worrying

about clothing coupons, and nylon stockings were available. Certain foods, such as sugar and tea, were still rationed, as were sweets. So life hadn't quite returned to normal even at that time which was seven years after the end of the war.

CHAPTER 16

MY MOVE TO EDINBURGH

Early September 1952, saw my friend and I arrive in the evening at Waverley Station, Edinburgh, complete with all our luggage. We soon found ourselves a taxi to transport us to the Simpson Memorial Maternity Hospital, which had the reputation of being one of the best in Scotland at the time.

It was a fairly new hospital, compared with the Edinburgh Royal Infirmary to which it was associated. The Royal was old fashioned with long stone corridors and the outside appearance was grey and dirty looking, with all the smoke of which Edinburgh was then famed.

The outlook from the front of the Simpson was quite pleasant, looking over the Meadows with grasslands and trees. The interior however, was cold looking, with lots of concrete slabs in the utility rooms. The nurses rooms were similar to those at the Aberdeen Royal, but had panel heating under the window, although the temperature was never very warm.

I remember the bedspreads were darkish blue green in colour, and the one in my room was not only not clean on my arrival, but had still never been washed or changed by the day I departed six months later!

We were supposed to go to the Royal for our meals

and also collect any mail, which was quite a distance, especially if it was cold and wet. As hospital standards go, the food was very good in taste, quantity and variety.

Unlike Aberdeen Royal, our lectures were given at different times of the day over the weeks, rather than in a block. This proved very tiring, especially if we were on night duty, as we were expected to get up twice sometimes during our sleeping time. There were times that you were in and out of uniform and pyjamas so often, you felt like a yo-yo!

We were even expected to attend lectures on our day off, while at other times we had to leave the wards, as while the lectures were on the agenda, we had usually eight to ten hourly talks per week. This often meant that you were eating meals during the day and also when on night duty, which tended to produce weight problems.

I remember one occasion when this was brought home to me, it was late evening and I had called a taxi to take me to Simpson's, after spending the weekend at home. The driver took me to the patients entrance, as he had taken me for a 'lady in waiting' - and he didn't mean the 'Royal' variety either, but the expectant kind! That caused a titter or two among my workmates!

The theory at Simpsons was first class, which is not surprising, as a lot of our lectures were given by the

Senior Sister Tutor, who had written an excellent book on midwifery. The practical side lacked opportunities however, so we had to practice with wooden box like structures with a round hole in the bottom, and soft doll like objects possessing all the wrong dimensions to appear natural.

We had to learn by heart a bit like the twelve times table, certain 'Passages', which is an appropriate word, as it describes the 'Route' a baby can take to be born, depending what position it is lying in, prior to the birth. We had to push, squeeze and pull these doll-like objects through the boxes and out through the circular hole, while reciting the appropriate words like an incantation. It all seemed like a playschool game, but was the nearest thing we had to reality.

In 1952-53 Caesarean births were few and far between at Simpsons, and babies born two weeks late were relatively common. I presume things have changed considerably since then.

The Special Nursery was often a busy place to be in during the night as the ill, premature and underweight babies were housed there, where the temperature was a constant 75 - 80 degrees. It was hot work, but the babies required the warmth.

The small babies were tube fed while some of those that were slightly heavier were bottle fed, until they reached a weight of five and a half pounds. At that time, if all was well, they were allowed home with their proud parents.

In those days, before medicine and technology was as advanced as it is now, we used to have what is called, Rhesus babies. Normally, the first born was unaffected, but subsequent babies developed jaundice a few days after delivery and they required what was called an 'Exchange Transfusion'.

For that procedure, the baby was placed on a padded mattress, with arms extended outwards. Small tubes, or catheters, were inserted in the babes arms, then, with a two-way syringe, twenty cc's of the babies blood was withdrawn. Immediately following that, twenty cc's of fresh blood was put into the baby. This procedure was continued until all the babies blood had been replaced with the fresh blood. It took more than an hour to complete this, with the whole procedure being strictly monitored.

If we were off duty during a morning or afternoon, we used to go down town to Princes Street, or the Bridges, and do some shopping, usually window shopping as we were invariably 'hard-up'.

We changed out of uniform into our out-door clothes and I remember that both the hems of our underskirts and dresses, and also our nostrils, were always black by the time we returned to the Nurses Home. This was because, in those days, there was no smokeless fuels and no restrictions on chimney emissions, so the air always seemed to be filled with black 'soot'.

There was also a lot of frost, so between the two it resulted in 'smog'.

I remember being in Edinburgh during the dreadful gales of 31st of January, 1953, which I understand was much worse up north. Haddo House Estate was one of the worst hit I believe, where a great number of trees were destroyed.

At Simpson's, there was pupil midwives from all parts of the world, with different accents and varying shades of skin, but everybody was friendly and I mixed with them well. I remember three Catholic girls from Dundee, who, probably being the least you would expect to do so, loved to hit the town on a Saturday night. Despite their 'excursions', they never failed to be up with the lark on a Sunday morning, then off to Mass, prior to being on duty at 7.30am.

Time was wearing on now and our exams were drawing near, which meant some frantic revision. The final days came and went, but this time, there was no celebration to follow. I think we were all too tired, the long hours combined with studying, had left us with no energy. In due course, the desired exam results arrived, then we packed our bags and said good-bye to Edinburgh at the end of February. I remember thinking that winter was not one of the best seasons to spend in the capital city.

CHAPTER 17

BACK TO ABERDEEN AGAIN

I had decided to take a few months off, before returning to Aberdeen Royal Maternity Hospital to do practical training, as the opportunity was better there.

However, my health was unexplainably under par and in December, I was rushed to hospital with a gangrenous appendix, which certainly explained my feelings of being unwell. I spent three weeks in hospital and after I was fully restored to good health, I continued my training. Some weeks later, I was off sick again, this time I had a kidney infection, but after investigation and treatment, I shortly returned to work.

We had to deliver at least ten babies under the supervision of a trained Midwife in the Labour Ward, before we went out 'On the District'. At that time, we lived in a house in Carden Place and if any expectant mums went into labour at any time, day or night, the Midwife in charge of the patient, would telephone and one of the District pupils had to attend. Depending on the urgency, we used the public bus or a taxi, the latter being preferred at night, for obvious reasons. Whether the call came form Torry, Mastrick, the town centre, etc, we had to hurry and join the Midwife.

When you were assisting in the delivery of a baby on district, you got your eyes opened and certainly saw ‘how the other half lived’.

In two locations, both of which have now been demolished and re-built, I remember that the first thing I noticed, was the wooden steps. These had been well worn with the constant wear of feet over the years and there was a quite a deep indentation on each step. This made the stairs quite tricky to negotiate in day light, but must have been much worse at night as there didn’t seem to be any lights.

When we got to the first of these calls, we discovered that there was little or no preparation for the new arrival, being only a minimum of clothes and bedding. There was no cot, so the new babes first bed was a drawer that we commandeered from a chest of them.

The other location was the old Castlehill Barracks, which was used as flats. They were three and four stories high and fronted with wrought iron railings. We arrived at 6am on a Saturday morning in the summer time. It was a lovely sunny morning and being early, there was nobody about. We were there for the best part of six hours before the baby was born.

The ladies husband was a crew member on a trawler and arrived in from the sea while we were there. By the time he arrived at the house, he was very much under the influence of drink. He started shouting and telling his wife to hurry up as he was needing out for more drink! In order to give her a little peace to get on with her 'labour of love', we had to lock him in a bedroom!

After we had made mum and the new baby as comfortable as we could amid the squalor, we were offered tea - in a jam jar. Despite the fact that we had had nothing to eat or drink since the night before and it was now noon, we declined, This refusal I have to say, was not so much because the 'tea-cup' was a jam jar, but more with the fact that the jar was particularly dirty. Needless to say, I have never developed either the inclination, or the knack, of drinking tea out of anything other than the average tea cup or mug!

We left the couple with their new arrival, their ninth no less, and returned for some much needed rest and refreshment. The following day, we returned to check on the health of both patients and we found the baby had bites all over it, from the bed bugs!

On another occasion, again very early in the morning, I arrived at a very nice terraced house with a lovely tidy garden. The Midwife was already there and the labour was progressing rapidly. It was soon evident that we would have to deliver two babies and not one, so the patient's doctor was informed and he arrived as the second baby was being delivered. All went very well, except that two of everything was required, instead of one. The parents were shaken but delighted.

When we delivered a baby on district, if the house

didn't have an open fire burning, we had to wrap the placenta, or afterbirth, in a parcel, or tin box, then bring it back to the Hospital with us by bus, so that we could dispose of it properly. I presume that this was in the interest of hygiene. Nowadays, I believe they are collected from Maternity Hospitals for export!!

After the medical students had studied for three years at the University, they started accompanying the Consultants on their rounds in the Wards throughout the Infirmary, to gain practical knowledge. They also visited the Labour Wards at the Maternity Hospital to witness the delivery of babies. When a delivery was imminent, the Labour Ward Sister would telephone the Residency, to alert the students.

This happened frequently during the night, and the students would arrive wearing pyjama's, or whatever was handy. Often they wouldn't arrive in time and I used to be sorry for the poor souls, dashing out in the middle of the night for nothing. I don't think students were too popular with the Ward Sister, who never seemed to allow them enough time after ringing, to make their night-dash in their pyjama's worth their while.

The budding doctors had to witness at least five normal births, also as many forceps deliveries and caesarean births as possible. This always seemed to me to be quite wrong and inadequate.

After they had delivered ten babies and witnessed the

others, it was these doctors we had to call out, if we were having to deal with complications. One thing they did learn however, was how to bath and dress a baby, as they had to perform these tasks for the babies they delivered. The majority of them became quite good at this, if nothing else!

After six months practical training, our group had to go to Dundee to sit our final exams, after which we would qualify to become State Registered Midwives. We all took a day trip to Dundee by train, which would have been fun if we hadn't been feeling all tensed up and apprehensive.

After the exams were over, there was no time left for shopping, as we had to dash to catch our train back to Aberdeen. There was nothing we could do then but sit and wait patiently for the results. I can't remember clearly, but I think we all passed. We were then entitled to add S.R.N. S.C.M. after our names.

I decided to stay on at Aberdeen Maternity Hospital as a Staff Midwife, while a few of the group went on to take further training in District Nursing. In Aberdeen, there were two big houses owned by the hospital, which had been converted into Maternity Homes. These, along with what had been a Fever Hospital, on the then perimeter of Aberdeen, were used for patients who were expecting second and subsequent babies, also others where no complications were anticipated.

It was now 1954 and in those days, the mums had to

stay in bed for a minimum of four days before they were allowed up. In these homes, the Labour Ward was on the ground floor, while nearly half the patients were one floor up and after delivery, the nurses had to carry the new mum up the stairs to the ward.

Though the two houses were commodious, the stairways were quite narrow, which meant that there was not enough room for three people to walk abreast. One nurse had to be either one step up or one step down, which was very hard on the poor old back, the actual degree of strain obviously depending on the weight of the patient.

Things are very different today, with some mums home on the day following their delivery, perhaps depending on the scarcity of beds. They seem to get on well, if not better, than they used to, by getting home sooner. Like all branches of medicine, there has been great advances made, which means that mums and babes are more likely to recover quickly, which is wonderful.

After a few months on days, I was put on night duty, along with two junior nurses. There was quite a rush from 9.30pm onwards as the babies all needed fed and settled for the night, before we got the mums comfy for their beauty sleep.

The babies weren't officially given feeds after midnight, instead they were given glucose and water, which wasn't always popular with the babes.

The idea being, that the babies were not encouraged to wake up during the night and get accustomed to a feed after they went home.

This was intended to be helpful to the mums when they went home at the end of the week, when they would be on their own 24 hours a day, which is exhausting if you continue to have broken nights sleep.

About that time, I bought a Morris Minor car for convenience. It was owned by a retired school teacher, who used it for a quick run to Banchory and back at the weekends. Though seven years old, it had only 14,000 miles on the clock, which in those days, you knew was genuine, there was no turning back of clocks then.

In September, a friend and I decided to be very adventureous and set off for the Braemar Gathering, which seemed quite a distance, but we got there in one piece. We had a methylated spirit stove, a kettle and a packed lunch, so were well prepared.

It was a dull, slightly dampish day, but we enjoyed ourselves and it seemed all too soon before it was time to head for home. There was one or two hiccups with the car on the way back, but we got home eventually, tired, but happy. That was the only time I ever attended the Gathering, so it was all the more memorable.

In the Autumn of 1954, I decided to sleep out, which meant renting a bed-sit. I located a room quite near to where I was working and on inspection, found an unmade bed, with a very cold, stone hot water bottle clearly visible.

The bed felt somewhat damp, which I presumed was just because it hadn't been in use for some time. I took the room and moved in. It had a small gas heater and ring that worked off an old penny meter, which proved a real pest, as it swallowed up the pennies at a terrific speed, so I frequently ran out of both heat and pennies.

As it turned out, the bed was indeed damp and meant the refilling of numerous hot water bottles in an attempt to dry it out. On my first day off, I went home and brought back a single bar electric fire, which was intended to be an improvement on the gas heater.

This arrangement however, didn't last more than twenty minutes, as it suddenly went off. Somehow, the landlady must have had a meter that she sat and studied and, perhaps may have seen me come in with my fire, whatever, she sure put paid to my idea of electric heating!

There was certainly nothing wrong with the electric fire, but it never worked in that flat again! After two weeks there, I caught a bad dose of the flu, so gave up the room and moved in with a friend at Holburn Junction.

In September of 1954, I had two weeks holiday. On the second last day, my parents and I went for a run in the car to Huntly and Insch, where we visited a lady and her family, who used to be a maid with us when I was a child. It was a lovely day and early harvesting was in progress.

We had taken my little Cairn Terrier dog with us and when we stopped the car just out of Ellon for a short time, the little fellow must have popped out unseen by us. When we got home it was dark, and to my horror, I discovered we had no dog. My father and I returned to Ellon, calling to enquire at the Police Station, but with no luck.

We then retraced our route, stopping the car near to where we had parked on our run, to my joy, we found the little fellow sitting by the roadside. That was very nearly one and a half hours he had remained patiently waiting there, he was indeed a welcome sight.

On the way home, I remember my father complaining of a painful heel and leg, but did not think much of it at that time. The next day, his leg was more painful and eventually, he allowed us to telephone the doctor. It was our own doctor's half day and in the late afternoon, a stand-in doctor arrived. He took one look at my dad, before asking if he could use our telephone and promptly phoned for an ambulance to take dad into Foresterhill Surgical Ward.

The doctor had diagnosed a serious condition called a 'Pulmonary Embolism'. I went into Aberdeen with my father and waited in the corridor until 2am, which was when he stabilised. After a few days, he was transferred to a Medical Ward.

He continued to have repeated thrombosis in the veins of his arms and legs, which required daily injections to thin his blood, the quantity depending on the daily results of his blood tests.

It was a very tiring and depressing time for him, as this procedure went on non-stop until around April, when his condition improved sufficiently to allow him to come home for a break, which helped to boost his moral. Unfortunately, within a fortnight, he was back in hospital.

During the two weeks at home, he had decided to go off for a short run in the car to visit old friends, he did not tell the family of his intention, with the result, we were all frantic till he came home. He seemed to want to prove to himself that he could still drive.

This was to be the last time he was ever at home and his condition fluctuated several times, before the added complication of a chest infection proved too much for him. He died on a Sunday morning in July

1955. I had gone on duty at 7.30am at the Private Maternity Home in Queens Road, to be told that the Night Sister had been trying to contact me during the night in order that I could summon the family, as my dad was dying, having deteriorated since visiting time the previous day.

We arrived at his bedside quickly, but he was only semi-conscious. I had to get permission from the Matron for a few days off, which was later extended to three months leave of absence.

Unfortunately, quite soon afterwards, my mother developed acute Arthritis and I had to give up my Midwifery, which consequently turned out to be permanent.

On my father's funeral day, a doctor cousin who was a great friend of the family, pleaded with me not to give up my profession. I only wish now, that I had fought harder to take his valuable advice as he knew my mother was a hypochondriac, as well as a selfish and self-centred person.

My father's death at the age of sixty, was the start of seventeen unhappy years for me. My father and I were very close and while he was in hospital for nine months, I visited him most days, often around 9am, before I went to bed after working a night shift. It became a routine visit he looked forward to.

As the weeks of his time in hospital went into months,

the senior doctors used to say ‘Good morning’, then pass him by. I suppose there wasn’t anything more they could do for him by then, but he used to feel very despondent at those times, it was as though he didn’t matter any more.

It was so sad, as he was always such a kind man and never complained. Nowadays, I suppose ‘Warfarin’, or ‘rat poison’, would have been prescribed to help him, as that acts by thinning the blood.

CHAPTER 18

THE WASTED YEARS

Being at home with my mother, I felt quite trapped so after a while, I bought a West Highland bitch puppy, as the Cairn Terrier had now died. After two years she had a litter of three puppies but unfortunately, only one was born alive, a lovely little girl. That however, was the real start of my life with dogs.

In June 1958, I felt so fed up with living at home that I booked two weeks holidays in the Channel Islands. I wanted to 'get away from it all', and went without leaving my address, in order that I could have complete peace for the fortnight. For that reason, I also chose to go alone.

By then I had four dogs, two of which were to be cared for at home, while the other two were put into boarding kennels on the outskirts of Aberdeen. I spent the night in Aberdeen and flew from Dyce to Manchester at 7am, where I had a four hour wait for a plane to Jersey, arriving at the hotel there at 6pm. It seems odd looking back, that it took a whole day for the journey, when nowadays you can fly half way round the world in about the same time.

I had a lovely week in Jersey, and flew to Guernsey for a second week. While there I had a day trip on a small boat to Sark then later on, a day trip to Herm. The weather was very like our summers here the week

I spent on Guernsey, but the week in Jersey was very warm and I returned more tanned than I have ever been in my life. The two weeks were extremely pleasurable and I returned home feeling suitably refreshed. At that time, little did I think that my trip to the Channel Islands would be the last holiday I would ever have to date, this being 1997 and thirty-nine years later.

Before I went on holiday I ordered one hundred point of lay pullets, these are six month old female chickens which are about to start laying eggs, thus becoming hens. They were free range reared and arrived in great condition. The breed was called Rhode Island Reds, which were very popular before poultry was all hybridised. They were unloaded into specially cleaned and prepared accommodation to give them every chance to do well and therefore prove profitable.

Unfortunately, six months after they were in full lay, they got a scare from some rats that were attracted by the food. This put the hens off their lay and from then on the profits dropped, despite my giving them expensive food designed to help them recover from the shock. Once they were no longer profitable, they then had to go. In those days, there were no firms like Rentokil to clear your premises of vermin, which would have perhaps prevented this incident.

I then decided to concentrate on dogs and puppies, and bought a passenger railway carriage for their accommodation. It was complete except for wheels, was sixty foot in length and nine foot wide. The carriage had to be cut in half for transportation and then craned onto two lorries, before being transported from Inverurie, where there used to be a loco works. The two halves were then lowered onto a level base and the joints sealed with roofing felt to make it watertight. It cost me £76 and the transportation cost, was I think, about £24.

It was a corridor carriage with seven compartments, plus two toilets. The interior had to be stripped of seats, racks and the brass rails across the corridor windows. There were water tanks, toilet and basins and even mirrors still intact, all of which had to be removed.

It was hard to believe that every piece of equipment and furnishings were fitted with solid brass screws. The carriage was certainly solidly constructed. It was well ventilated and made ideal kennels, though heat was required in the winter.

I added gradually a few Beagles, which are super dogs with excellent temperaments. If given the chance to escape however, they quickly demonstrated the fact they were scent hounds, as they would take off at great speed, following their noses which led them to only they knew where!

They were mainly tri-colour, which is black, a mahogany brown and white, with the saddle being black and shiny. Their chest, lower legs, tummy and half tail was white with other parts being rich brown. They were not particularly obedient, you would have really thought that they were deaf as they tended to please themselves, but in my eyes, they were beautiful. My first one was six months old when I bought her and I loved her, as I did all of my Beagles, they were all special in their own way.

Thc Beagles were very popular as they required little or no grooming because of their short hair. When I advertised a litter, the puppies were always in great demand, but I used to put prospective buyers through the third degree to make sure they would make suitable owners.

This was partly because, if Beagles started to escape on a regular basis, owners would get fed up with them. Left to their own devices, there was then a danger that they would be picked up and end up in research laboratories. In these laboratores, they would be strapped to smoking machines and used for experiments. One very cruel and well-known practice was when they were forced to inhale smoke at the equivalent of thirty cigarettes daily. This was done over a period of two to three years, before the dogs were killed and their lungs examined for cancer.

The tobacco companies already knew full well both the damage cigarettes did to lungs and the danger smoking presented to human beings, though they would not admit it.

It made me extremely angry how badly Beagles were treated in the name of 'Medical Research'. Beagles are an exceptionally trusting breed and even when hurt or ill, you could do anything to them and they would never bite, however much discomfort they were suffering.

As with any animal, they deserved the best of homes and I preferred to sell a puppy to a retired, or semi-retired couple who liked walking a lot, then they fitted in perfectly. I once sold a puppy to a Minister from near Elgin, who visited his parishioners on his bicycle and cycled twenty to twenty five miles daily, taking a packed lunch for himself and the dog.

He returned to visit me two years later and I have never seen such a happy, fit and healthy specimen, with muscles on his legs like iron. I mean the dog of course, not the minister!! He wanted a second Beagle but that proved to be a mistake as they tended to take off together, whereas his first dog had been content to stay at home after his daily run.

Once two young lads on an angling holiday were camping in one of the fields near the house, they tended to fish at night and sleep during the day. My Beagle had gone to investigate the new arrivals and she returned with one of their caps, proving to be quite a retriever, which is not typical of a scent hound.

A few days later, I was presented with a fair-sized whole fish which the lads had intended to eat for their supper after they had awakened from their sleep. Apparently they had stored the fish in their tent and she had poked her head under the canvas and 'retrieved' it for me. The lads luckily treated the affair as a joke and I substituted their fish with fresh eggs, so they did not starve.

Beagles are not given 'doggy' names, they have what is known as hound names. One bitch I bred and kept for myself was called Melody, she was about sixteen inches in height which is standard for the breed, tri-coloured, with a wonderful nature.

Once she was an age for it, I also bred from her. When she was in 'whelp' or pregnant, her girth grew as the days passed, to the extent that she had me worried. About ten days before she was due, there was an advert in the daily paper offering a Springer Spaniel as a foster mother. She had had a 'mis-alliance' which resulted in an unwanted litter and the owners planned to put the puppies down at birth.

The Spaniel was young so maybe would require some help during the birth. The owner expected to be away from home on business at that time and there was no one available that she considered competent enough to cope. I contacted the owner and within a couple of days, the Spaniel had settled in with me.

She had her puppies first, five cross Spaniels that she was quite happy with and a few days later, Melody had a litter of twelve puppies, all healthy and of equal size. After she had settled for a few hours, I removed four of her puppies and switched them for four of the Spaniels, having first sponged the Beagles and the one remaining Spaniel pup with diluted Dettol so they would all have the same smell, in order to confuse the mother Spaniel. This way she would hopefully accept them as her own as it has been known for dogs to kill and eat strange puppies.

All went well for both mothers, the only unfortunate thing being, I had to take the cross puppies to the vet to be put down, as was the owners wish. It was a horrible thing to have to do, but was carried out properly and painlessly.

At the end of eight weeks, both litters were fully weaned and all thirteen puppies were re-united. The Spaniel puppy found a good home and the mother was returned fit and well to her owner.

The twelve beagle puppies were later photographed in a straight line in a trough-like construction, they were standing on their hind legs with their front paws on the trough. It was a split second pose which we were very lucky to capture with such lively youngsters, as all other attempts had only showed eleven or less puppies.

My Beagles were well known and appreciated, ending up in homes all over Britain, from the North of Scotland to the south of England. I also showed Shetland Sheepdogs and West Highland terriers, but being longer-haired, they took a lot of preparation over the weeks previous to a show to get their coats in good condition and trim.

This took more time than I could always spare, so consequently I was not so successful with those two breeds. It was all good fun however, and a chance to re-unite friendships with other breeders and see what they were producing.

Throughout the years, I also had a few poodles of different colours. My first being Sally, a biggish miniature. She was dark silver in colour with a white bit on her chest, so she was described as mis-marked. Like the great majority of poodles, she was extremely affectionate and clever.

After a few years, she decided she was going to spend each night on my bed instead of her own bed in the warm kitchen. She just had to see me lift a hot water bottle to fill it, and that was the signal for her to mount the stairs and jump onto my bed. She would then make herself comfortable in the centre, thereby making things more than a little uncomfortable for me, as she soon felt quite heavy on your legs. Sally incidentally lived to be sixteen and a half, despite latterly having a heart condition.

Being at home with my mother was not exactly my idea of life, especially after the enjoyable years of nursing, so had it not been for the two way love and affection between my dogs and myself, I don't think I could have coped. As I have said previously, my mother and I had never hit it off, not even when I was a child.

Mainly to break the monotony of my life, I attended several evening classes over the years I was at home. As I had left school so early, I started with Commercial English and Maths to improve my general education. Next came basket making, and I still have two of the baskets I made, after forty years.

One of my projects was to make a dog basket, which I thought I was doing very well with, until it came to putting in the 'door' at the front. No matter how I tried, I could not seem to get the right shape for the front. However, never daunted, I re-designed the dog basket without a curved opening at the front, so setting a new personal fashion in canine beds!

I also tried pottery, which was fun, but could be very messy, before I ended up my 'range' of courses at that time with car maintenance, which I thought would come in handy.

One Saturday, a month after my father died in July 1955, I had all four wisdom teeth removed in Foresterhill under general anaesthetic. On the afternoon following the extractions, I was given a cup of tea, and to my horror, all the liquid ran out of one side of my mouth.

It transpired I had Bells Palsy, or in other words, a

paralsyed face. I was still discharged on the Monday as planned and drove home alone in my car.

At the end of that week our family doctor sent me in to see a neurologist, and I was admitted to the nurses' ward as, though on leave, officially I was still on the staff. I was under observation for about a week, and during that time, I experienced migraine for the first time, which was much worse than my face problems.

After about a month, my face returned to ninety-five per cent of what it was before. At that time, little did I think it would return twenty years later. The second time around I was given Cortizone, the side effects of which, I still have to cope with to-day.

After the trauma of my fathers death, closely followed by my teeth extractions and my face problem, I developed a strange collection of symptoms and fatique which over thirty years later was to be diagnosed as Myalgic Encephalomyelitis or ME. There was scant knowledge of ME in the fifties, nobody knew what it was and therefore could give little sympathy, though the sufferers were frequently unwell.

There is still no cure, and after forty years, I have learned to live with it. When I am tired, I rest, when I feel better however, the natural thing to do is overdo it, I then become overtired and pay for it over the next few days. You can see a broken leg in plaster, but you can't see ME. Over the years it's been a case of, if ill, try all the different types of complimentary medicines, vitamins and minerals, and, above all, make the best of it.

Speaking of teeth, reminds me of one winter around nineteen sixty, when following my suffering a lot of toothache again, it was arranged that I should have quite a few extractions under general anaesthetic in the local hospital. On the appointed day, our farm road was dyke high with snow, so I was transported to the main road, through a field by a tractor, where I was met by car.

For some reason I had decided to come round from the anaesthetic before I should have done and I can remember struggling frantically, before the ether was switched full on to knock me out again. The other patients who had teeth out that day were on their way home by the time I woke up from my double dose of Ether. I incidentally, was as sick as the proverbial dog!! I finally got home late afternoon, again sitting holding on like grim death to the inside of the tractor, and still feeling very sick. For days afterwards, I remember still having the smell and taste of ether in my mouth.

Over the years, my mother began to require more attention than I could give her, partly because of the dogs, and partly because of the effects of ME. My family kept telling me to 'get rid of the dogs', as they were obviously 'too much', but I had no intention of giving in, I felt I had given up enough. My mother was eventually moved to a Residential Home where she died within a year, at the age of eighty two.

By that time, there was mumblings within the family. A year before my mother died, certain steps had been taken behind my back, that affected my inheritance, though I knew nothing of that till later.

It was now early December 1972 and I was more or less given six months to move out of the only home I had ever known. Verbal communication was practically non-existent, and nasty tricks were played on both myself, and the dogs in the kennels, eg lighting and heating was tampered with, to the extent it placed their lives in danger.

I started looking in earnest for a new home that would be suitable for myself and my canine family to move into. I scanned properties in the papers and viewed crofts over a wide area. Finally, I negotiated for a farmhouse and steading that had just under one acre of ground. It had been vacant for two years except for the storing of some furniture in the loft. After several weeks of haggling, I became the owner of the property in the middle of February.

The house required some repairs and the minimum necessary to make it habitable was duly carried out. The steading was a different matter altogether. There was what was called a single byre capable of holding sixteen cows. The wooden partitions of which, were old and rotting, so all were removed.

There was a new tax coming into force at the end of March, called VAT which added 8% to the cost of raw materials. This meant a detailed list of requirements had to be made quickly to avoid the extra expenditure. The list included things like cement blocks for kennel partitions etc. I also required over one hundred, eight foot high fence posts, with eighteen rolls of six and four feet high, chain link fencing, heavy duty and galvanised for durability.

I bought metal gates at an Auction sale, and they had to be transported to a local Blacksmith, six at a time in my mini-van, to have heavy hinges welded on to them, so that they could be cemented on to the concrete partitions. There was also wood, plaster board, nails, staples etc, etc. It amounted to quite a lot, but I met the deadline before the end of March, so avoiding paying the new VAT tax on materials.

While I was waiting for all the above to arrive, I was busy organising the leaving of my old home, and the selling of any furniture etc, which I wouldn't have room for in my new home. Also, I badly needed the ready cash for payment of my purchases. Some of the family heirlooms had to go, which was not easy, and though disappointed, I had no choice, as I had to manoeuvre within a tight budget.

I had six tradesmen, or very handy 'handymen' carrying out the alterations to the steading, who worked like trojans nearly every Saturday afternoon and Sunday. As well as constructing the kennels, a kennel kitchen was made, in what used to be the stable. An isolation unit was then made next door to the kitchen.

The railway carriage, previously mentioned, was also moved, along with two large wooden kennels. All were craned on to lorries, transported and craned off on arrival at their new sites. After that was completed, a perimeter fence was erected, the supporting posts being cemented two feet into the ground. Fencing dividing the dog runs was then erected and finally, all the gates were made and put into place. The bulk of the work was then completed, except for finishings to the kitchen and the required electrical work still to be carried out.

Some days, I paid several visits to the new kennels and each time I transported something with me, for example a carpet, which I would lay before I returned. I also started moving some of my older dogs, as the removal date of the end of May was rapidly approaching. This meant double work, as I had dogs in both places to care for several times daily.

All the time my work team were at the new kennels, I transported cooked food every Saturday and Sunday. Despite having ME, I must have had an awful lot of adrenalin circulating in my system, as somehow - somehow, I managed to cope. Looking back, I often wonder how, as the work involved, between the end of February and the end of May was beyond belief!!

A relative helped me to pack the glassware, crockery, china and ornaments and all the etc's. Her family also moved the portable kennels with a tractor and bogie, which was a great help. As I took down curtains, I washed them right away, so that they were ready to put up in my new home, which was much smaller than my present one, being a two up, two down, complete with; bathroom, kitchen, pantry and front porch, the latter being a wonderful sun trap.

The removal was set for a Friday at 1pm and the van arrived on time. There was however, a problem when a member of my family proved once again, to be his devious self, by going into the house the previous night, presumably through a window, before leaving by the front door, locking it and taking the key with him.

The removal men had planned to use the front door as it was easier for negotiating the bigger items of furniture. They were not daunted however by the missing key as they promptly went and demanded that my relative hand it over. They duly returned with the key and reported they had obtained it without blows. All went smoothly after that, and on Saturday am, they returned for some things which they hadn't had room for on the previous afternoon.

The difficult family member insisted that they take a heavy cast iron mangle with them. It was still in good working order, but with washing machines in everyday use, was by then redundant. The men decided they had better do as they were told to avoid any further words.

The mangle was then perched on to the back of their lorry and so journeyed through the town on a busy Saturday morning. The sight must have caused a bit of amusement.

The removal men said they would take it home with them, dismantle it and sell it as scrap. Nowadays, of course it would probably be a valued antique. It's amazing what a few years can do for supply and demand, not to mention value. That applied to all the big furniture I had to part with.

In mid March while the railway carriage was being craned off, I couldn't bear to look, and instead, I planted some roses I had bought for my new garden. By the time the craning operation was completed, my roses were happily installed.

CHAPTER 19

MY NEW HOME

It was now springtime, 1973, with good temperatures and quite dry, which helped the vegetables that someone had planted in my garden for me. The top growth of the potatoes was about three feet high, which normally would signal a poor yield, but despite that, they were a great crop of huge potatoes.

The garden had been fallow for several years so it was almost virgin soil, very sandy, with gravel about nine inches down. This meant it dried out quickly and was greedy as regards fertilisers. It also didn't particularly suit the roses, which tended to struggle.

Soon after I moved in, I bought two hundred fir and pine trees from an estate, and they were planted where they were likely to give maximum shelter. They didn't have the best of starts, as the summer was particularly dry, and they had to be watered with whatever water was available.

Because I had my own water supply in the form of a well, I couldn't be too liberal, as I wasn't sure how the supply would hold out if the dry weather was to continue for any length of time. Quite a few of the trees didn't survive in the end and those that did tended to bend with the wind as they grew older. This was caused, not only by a lack of water, but by a combination of the gravelly sub soil and the shallow roots of the trees. I also planted lots of daffodils in the garden, as well as amongst the trees at the gate, these did prosper and looked lovely in Spring.

From the early days, I had decided to use the newly converted part of the kennels as boarding kennels as at that time, there wasn't another in the area, and overseas holidays were becoming increasingly popular. There was also a fair number of people moving into the area with the advent of the oil industries and the building of the power station.

Through word of mouth, and recommendation from local vets, business soon began to increase, especially through July and August. Easter and Christmas were also good times for business, but of course cancellations could occur at Christmas if the weather proved stormy, and plans had to be then changed.

Looking after other peoples dogs was quite different from looking after ones own, as they were sometimes homesick if they had never been left before, especially if they were that bit older. The majority of the younger ones however, were usually delighted to have new company to romp around with.

Food wasn't much of a problem, as I always asked what they normally ate and when, and what was their favourites. Another important question I asked was, "What do you say to the dog to take them out to spend a penny?" You wouldn't believe some of the answers I used to get and the things I ended up having to shout, but it did save standing around for ages on a cold night!

I also encouraged the owners to bring the dogs own beds, blankets and toys into the kennels, so that they had something familiar with them, which had a smell of home. Over the years, I really didn't have a great many problem dogs.

Some came so often that they used to get very excited when they turned into the end of the road three-quarters of a mile from the kennels. Those dogs were usually the ones who ignored their owners when they returned to collect them. It could be quite amusing at times.

When anybody new phoned to book their dog in, I always asked what breed of dog they had and used to squirm if they said Labrador cross, particularly if it was with a Collie. They were usually bundles of energy twenty four hours a day and barked a lot. Other problems were the odd one that cleared six foot fencing, I remember one Boxer in particular who was an expert at it. It certainly paid me to remember this idiosyncrysy if that dog was coming to stay!

It was now 1973 and my first Autumn in my new home. On the 7th October, although it seems almost unbelievable, I rose to discover that I had suddenly been transported into a winter landscape. We had had so much snow earlier that morning that by mid-day, my long road was blocked with wreaths of snow.

I remember it was a Tuesday, because that was the day the bakers van called, on this occasion however, we obviously had no bread delivered as the van could not get through.

The following day, a friend left bread for myself and my neighbour at the end of the road, and though we had to trek through the snow to collect it, we were very grateful for the gift. That particular snow storm meant I was snowed in for ten days that October and I wondered what I had let myself in for! This episode did however serve to teach me a valuable lesson, to always ensure that I had plenty of food in stock, for both myself and the animals!

In winter after the snow had been lying on the ground for several days, the courtyard became a solid sheet of ice as a result of so many cars turning. More than once I had had some nasty falls, resulting in an injury to my back. This usually meant coping as best as I could until the inflammation died down, before a visit to the Osteopath to put matters right.

On one occasion, I had been for manipulation and received the usual instructions, "Do as little as possible for three days, and no lifting." On arrival home late afternoon, I had my tea, then changed into my working clothes in preparation for feeding the dogs. I got to the kennel kitchen, and to my horror, I had had a delivery of dog food, all twenty bags of it and every one heaped up in my kennel kitchen, preventing me working there.

I had no option then but to get a sack barrow, set to and move the food, one bag at a time to the store, where it should have been left in the first place! It was not the usual lorry driver, or the mistake would not have happened. By the time I was finished, my back problem was back to square one, till a second manipulation was given two weeks later.

Sometime later, I injured an ankle, probably doing something I shouldn't have been doing! Anyway, it continued to give me trouble for some time and I was told to go to the local hospital to have it X-Rayed, in case I had broken a bone. I had an appointment and was cutting things a bit close for time, so I hurriedly washed, then changed my clothes.

Although I had had a bath the previous evening, my

feet were dirty after feeding the animals wearing my wellies that morning. To save time, I inserted the 'offending' foot into the wash basin and scrubbed it whilst hopping about on my other leg. I made it to the X-Ray Department in time by the skin of my teeth, and promptly broke out in a cold sweat, when it dawned on me that the Radiologist may require me to remove both shoes for the X-Ray! Thankfully, my embarrassment was spared, but I have never again cut such corners in an effort to beat 'Old Father Time'!!

After a couple of years, I added a six month old goat kid and some bantam poultry to my growing 'menagarie'. I had to be careful not to let the bantams out when the dogs were runnung about as town dogs weren't used to fluttering feathers and would kill them if the opportunity arose.

The goat though very petted, could look after herself and did so, with horned head ever at the ready. She was however, an awful 'baby' when it came to water as she couldn't 'thole' being out in a shower of rain, even mist would cause her to roar incessantly and this would continue until she was taken inside.

After a few years, I became aware that some of my customers had cats as well as dogs, when one said to me, having dropped off his dog, that he was then about to take his cat to a cattery. I thought to myself "That's stupid, I could convert the loft into a cattery", and that's what I proceeded to do - myself.

I ordered three foot high weld mesh wire, which was sold in twenty five metre rolls. I also got about two dozen sheets of thick chipboard, there was plenty of wood around to make doors and after buying a supply of hinges, bolts and staples, I was ready to go.

I made three pens so that they would be ready for the July Trades Fortnight, a popular holiday time. I made the pens in the evenings after tea and worked for a few hours solid as I had good lights to see what I was doing. The first three pens were the smallest, but varied in size, from four by four feet to four by six feet.

Both the owners and the cats alike appreciated them being so spacious, and the cats got plenty of exercise, climbing up the wire partitions. As the years passed, I added other pens until they were lined up both sides of the loft, with a wide passage up the middle for access. The later pens were bigger, up to ten feet long, which proved useful as several customers had up to three or four cats and preferred them to be housed together. The loft tended to be warm in summer, but with opening doors at both ends, the ventilation was good.

I enjoy joinery work and of necessity gained plenty of practice, so I became quite good at it. My kennels and cattery were mentioned in a Good Kennel and Cattery Guide in the 1980's, which I was very proud of as there were only ever a few in the Grampian area mentioned.

In the early days when money was tight, I considered taking an evening job to earn a little extra cash and upon seeing an advertisement in the newspaper for a 'Betterware' salesperson, I applied by telephone. The person I had to contact was out and I was asked to phone back later, in the meantime I was having second thoughts.

When I called back, I said to the gentleman concerned, "I don't really think I am the person you are looking for, because if I called at a house where there were several young children and obviously money was scarce, I would probably say to the lady of the house not to bother as she could perhaps buy whatever she was interested in, a lot cheaper in Woolworths." He thanked me for calling and agreed that I may not be the most suitable person for the job!!

I also harboured thoughts about evening work in a

fish factory, but didn't particularly fancy handling cold wet fish, under cold wet running water and standing in wellingtons on a cold wet floor. So I also decided against that. Thankfully for any prospective employers, I subsequently survived the lean period without ever finding my 'niche' in alternative employment.

As I got busier, I put an advert in the local paper for a school boy or girl to work Saturdays and holidays and was suprised to receive thirty two replies. One girl replied the evening the paper was published and she sounded very bright and enthusiastic, but as the paper was not generally for sale until the following morning, I said I would have to wait and see who else applied, before I could make a decision.

Bright and early next morning, the very enthusiastic young lady was on the phone again; "Well do I take it I have got the job?" To which I replied she had, deciding she deserved it for her enthusiasm, if nothing else! She proved to be a very quick and efficient worker, and had a great way with the dogs, being quite fearless.

She was with me for a period of years and sometimes in summer, she would come to work on the back of her own horse, which would then graze happily until she was ready to go home again. One summer, both her horses were with me for two weeks and ate down my grass, which was handy as it saved me cutting the runs with a mower. That young lady is still a great friend and remains involved with animals, though now married with a family.

As I had two rooms which I didn't use, I decided to try and let them furnished. A girl answered the advertisement saying she would like them for her boyfriend who was at sea and would only be ashore at weekends. After viewing the rooms she decided to take them, and on the Saturday afternoon arrived rather unexpectedly to do his washing!! After using all of my hot water, she then gaily departed, saying she would be back later.

Return she duly did, and proceeded to cook his Sunday dinner, before again departing saying her boyfriend would be in later. Around midnight both arrived and to my horror the 'cook cum washerwoman' was supporting the boyfriend, who was stone drunk. I took one look at him and said "No way are you staying in this house in that state, or any other state, so you had better depart and take your clean washing and cooked dinner with you." Thankfully they departed in peace, but that incident taught me a lesson, which ensured that I was very careful in my choice of other tenants in the future.

In the mid seventies, I bought an old twenty two foot caravan which I intended to use as a grooming room, but soon after, a local gentleman who was convalescing after his discharge from hospital, experienced problems at home due to his lack of mod cons. I therefore had the caravan painted and furnished, then a gas cooker and fire were installed. The caravan was quite comfortable and warm, so I invited the gentleman to stay.

He had health problems so a little supervision was necessary. He was also in need of some warm clothing and this I was able to acquire at jumble sales at a low cost. I made sure that he had food, clean clothing and access to a regular bath. He was with me for just under a year before moving to a sheltered home, by which time he was in much better health.

Over the years I had employed several boys and girls but only one ever worked for me full time. Some were employed under the Government Job Scheme aimed at giving youngsters experience, which the majority enjoyed, though the odd one or two were not interested and therefore not very satisfactory. The last girl I had was excellent and also a keen gardener. She is still involved with animals and her own garden, but has now added oil painting to her hobbies.

After a few years, I had to arrange times for customers to bring in and collect their animals, as people were turning up at odd times of the day including mealtimes. Sundays also began to present a problem, as some people just arrived un-announced to see the animals. They were usually accompanied by several screaming children who ran in all directions, scaring the living daylights out of the animals. It sometimes took some explaining to these people that I did not own a ZOO.

On one occasion, some children hit a kennel with a ball with such force, they scared and upset a mother with puppies so much, that three puppies ended up being killed by their mother, who was jumping frantically up and down in her bed. That proved very upsetting for the dog, not to mention what it did to me and put the final seal on the Sunday escapades. I then started closing all day on Sunday's, in order to give both the animals and myself a bit of peace.

One of my regular customers had a Labrador dog as well as a cat and when she went on holiday, her animals came to stay with me. This time however, pussy had three kittens, all pure white and absolutely beautiful. The problem was, they were only ten days old, their eyes barely open and too young to be vaccinated. I had to keep them as far away from the other cats as possible, to protect them from any possible infections.

They got on very well and when the owner returned to collect them, I asked her if she had homes for the kittens and was delighted when she said no. I decided to have one and was duly given first choice. I chose the one with the squarest face and she took up residence with me when she was ten weeks old.

She had a fluffy white coat, so the first name chosen for her was 'Fluffy', but that was too plain for such a beautiful cat, so I decided to call her 'Beethoven', as some white cats can occasionally be deaf! Lots of people thought this name highly amusing, not too say, a little strange. At the time of writing, she is enjoying her afternoon nap under my duvet, at the grand age of eleven.

I had always had pet dogs in the house, sometimes up to three at a time. Some were house dogs from puppies, while others gravitated from being in the kennel when young, to moving into the house upon their retirement. In the middle eighties, nature had taken its course and the house was very quiet and empty.

Soon afterwards, I had a litter of chocolate brown puppies, which were the result of an 'accident', as a marriage had not been arranged, at least, not by me! The mum produced six puppies, five brown and a black one, which was sadly, still-born. There were three normal sized puppies and two very small ones, obviously premature, indicating that she had mated twice.

I hurriedly took the two tiny, almost hairless, puppies into the house, put them immediately into a box, before placing it into the bottom of the warm oven, with the door left wide open. I then organised a more permament bed for the babies using a special electric blanket, so they were kept at a constant temperature. After they dried off and settled down, I checked on the other three puppies, mum and babies were all fine.

My next job was to look out the hand-rearing equipment, which I had had for the best part of twenty years. I had to keep a good supply of teats and valves handy, as once used they perished. The teats were only available from the original suppliers of the equipment in London. Feeding with a special preparation proved a little difficult to begin with, but the two babes soon got the hang of what they had to do.

I had to be careful not to feed them too quickly as milk could come down their little noses, or make them splutter as if choking. Then I had to wipe their faces to prevent the hair getting hard and uncomfortable, whilst not forgetting the other end!

This was most important, as their bed needed to be kept scrupulously clean, a procedure normally attended to by the mother licking them clean. It was also a means of checking whether they had properly digested their food, or if they had diarrohea, or constipation. Either condition would mean that I would need to quickly adjust their diet.

They were fed as frequently as I had time for, approximately every two to three hours to begin with, both day and night. Unfortunately, when they were ten days old, the little boy, the bigger of the two, died, leaving the small girl on her own. As time went on, she started to make better progress, and at eight weeks old, the night feeds could be stopped, thankfully. Bottle fed puppies and kittens are generally slow to accept solid food, and my little friend was no exception.

When she was twelve weeks old, she started her course of vaccinations, and at sixteen weeks old, she was ready to face the big wide world - and adult dogs. She had only been accustomed to me up to that time, so had never seen older dogs, consequently she was petrified. Throughout her whole life, she never really grew to enjoy the company of other dogs, always remaining a little apprehensive.

At about four months old, she started taking fits, so I had to keep her as quiet as possible. The fits were at first thought to be connected to her teething, but as time went on, they continued and medication was a case of trial and error. Things didn't improve, and quite by chance, I was given the name of a Homeopathic Vet, south of Glasgow.

After a telephone conversation, he sent me pills to give her and I was to let him know how she responded. Several times over a period of a month, the medication was changed, depending on her reactions, for better or worse, till eventually, she stablised. She ended up taking three different pills every morning, which she remained on all her life, though as she got older, the fits did become a lot less frequent and severe.

Being hand fed, she became very dominant, as all hand fed animals tend to be, so I wrote to an animal behaviourist about her. He gave me instructions to the effect that I should always keep her in the background rather than by me, as she had become the leader of the pack, instead of me! This turned out to be too difficult for me to reinforce as she is such a small lady, whom I always felt had missed out on a proper 'doggy' family life. I'm afraid therefore, that I tended to continue to give in to her dominance!

Bonny is her name and she is now thirteen years old, unfortunately, for the past two years, she has suffered from blindness. I suspect this to be a result of continuely banging her fragile skull during her fits. She has however, become quite adept at finding her way around in her dark world, as long as I do not move any furniture etc. A growing deafness also adds to her problems, meaning she requires a fair bit of looking after.

As a result of her ill health, I have only ever been separated from her for two nights during a stay in hospital, in all of her thirteen years. A Poodle loving neighbour looked after her during this time and I arrived home to find her with a tummy upset which was caused by her stress over my 'disappearance'. When I acquired Beethoven, I thought her arrival would benefit Bonny by providing her with a companion, but though they became friends, Bonny always remained my 'Baby'.

I had planted two apple trees at the kennels which blossomed at the same time, so pollinating each other. They took a few years to get properly established and provide apples that were of a reasonable size and quantity. However, the Autumn arrived when there was a reasonable crop and I decided to have a go at making cider.

I think the recipe I used was from Jimmy Young's radio show. The apples had to be washed and chopped roughly, unpeeled, then water and sugar was added and the whole concoction needed to be stirred daily for a given time. At some time, lemon juice had to be added, but unfortunately, I didn't have a fresh lemon and once again, the road was blocked with snow. I therefore used instead, the juice of a 'plastic' lemon, which contains a preservative. The contents of the containers were then strained carefully into screw top bottles.

After the recommended time for storage was passed, I checked the bottles. Though the cider was a little cloudy at the bottom of the bottles, it tasted very good and proved to have quite a kick in it! One bottle was forgotten about and left un-opened for several years. Unfortunately, unlike Whisky, my brew did not improve with keeping, turning out to be totally undrinkable.

Speaking of my cider, reminds me of an elderly Ward Sister who used to make ginger beer and lemonade for her patients. When I was on night duty in the hospital, one night, following a warm day, the gas in one of the bottles built up with the heat and it exploded with a loud bang. The bottle was stored on a patient's locker at the time and the flying glass resulted in him requiring stitches. You could say that this particular gentleman had a very rude awakening!

During the Autumn and Winter of 1985, my health was giving me increasing problems. This caused my ME to grow worse, a condition I had now suffered from for thirty one years. I got to the stage where I couldn't stand the cold, wet days when I had to be out, as the animals had to be attended to, whether I liked it or not. I was eventually forced to make the decision to sell up and retire early. It was a sad end to what had been both an interesting and happy time in my life. During my time in the kennels, I had experienced the satisfaction felt from the hard work involved in setting up a business with nothing.

I had had the pleasure of meeting a lot of kind people and their, not always well-behaved, but invariably well-loved and interesting animals. These people were extremely appreciative of both my own and my helpers efforts in making their pets stay with us, as comfortable as was humanly possible. I would miss them all with a great sadness.

In May 1986, I put the kennels on the market, and through the weekly dog magazines, soon had eight people interested, who came from Inverness to the Midlands of England. The kennels was finally sold with an entry date in August. I had a lot to arrange before then, including finding myself somewhere to live in town. That proved fairly easy as lots of suitable properties were on the market at the time. My greatest problem would be finding suitable homes for some of my animals.

The new owner had agreed to keep my hens and ducks, along with the two cats who lived in the buildings and kept the place free of mice very efficiently. My 'rain-shy' goat went to live with a friend who already had two goats and she settled in quite happily. I also found homes for a few of the younger dogs, but the older ones were a problem.

Sadly, it became necessary for eight dogs to be put down, some of which were my beloved Beagles, who would not have settled into new homes, partly because of their age and breed, but also as they were not house trained. It was a very sad and traumatic day when the Vet came to put them to sleep, I remember shaking like a leaf, both before, and for a very long time afterwards.

Bonny and Beethoven were coming with me on my moving day and I left four dogs behind temporarily, intending them to follow on later. Of those, three of them were given to what I thought was a good home. Unfortunately, it proved to be anything but, as when I called over the next few months to see how they were getting on, I found, to my horror, that they were wrecks. I returned with food for them and after a while, they seemed to improve, but I continued to remain uneasy and worried about them.

One finally escaped during a severe snow storm and was never seen again. Another died and the third I eventually rescued, with the help of a neighbour. She was in a shocking condition, soaking wet, shivering and very smelly, having been left with no bedding, she also had a kidney infection. An animal cruelty officer later visited the place with me and after a strong verbal warning, advised the owners from keeping any more animals, I hope for any animal's sake, they took his advice.

I now had three dogs which was a handful, but at least they would live and end their lives in comfort. If only I could have lived those three months once again, I would have had those three dogs put to sleep, as however painful it would have proved to be for me, at least they wouldn't have had to suffer needlessly!

As August approached, there was a lot of packing and tidying up to be done. It was also the busiest time for boarders, so my helper and I didn't have to look far for a job. The grass seemed to grow faster than ever and had to be cut regularly to keep the place looking tidy. The fruit in the garden was ripe, so had to be picked and jam made, or some frozen. It was definitely all systems go, inside and out.

I got the keys for the new house a week before the day I was due to move, which helped, as suitcase after suitcase, box after box, could then be taken over and unpacked. I had to decide to leave some big wardrobes behind for the new owners as the staircase in my present house was S-shaped and had proved a major obstacle to installing large furniture when I moved in. I remember the wardrobes had been pushed, pulled and heaved up a ladder by four strong men, through a window removed for the purpose, before they could successfully get them where they should be. There was no way I was attempting to demolish fixtures to take them out again!

When the removal men arrived, I felt quite sad, as I was leaving what was really my first home, but on the other hand, I was quite aware that I was not physically fit to carry on any longer. I left Bonny and Beethoven at the old house until the evening, before collecting them and taking them to their new domain once the stir was over so that they could then explore in peace.

CHAPTER 20

MY RETIREMENT IN TOWN

My first night of retirement in August 1986, proved to be rather a restless one, as I had a hospital appointment the next morning, involving the first of six tests to try and unravel the mystery of my health problems. The instructions I had received from the hospital had stipulated no food or drink from the previous night, which meant no comforting tea to ease my worries.

At the end of the next day, I was none the wiser. The tests continued for six months, and succeeded in ruling out a number of possibilities, including Brucellosis, but failed to get to the route of my problems. The specialist said to me, 'Go home and look after yourself!'

Shortly after that time, I picked up a magazine in the local Supermarket and printed on the front cover, were the words; 'The mystery illness that the Doctor's don't understand.' I told my GP about the contents of the article, and asked him if that was my problem, he said yes. At least, after thirty years, I knew. When my Doctor finally confirmed that I had ME, it was a great relief, as there is nothing so frightening as the fear of the unknown, even though, there is as yet, no cure. You just have to learn to live with it.

After leading a very active life for so long, sitting around, 'taking it easy' only made me feel restless, so

I decided to look for some charity work. I didn't have long to wait before I saw an article about Pet Fostering in Scotland. I made enquiries and a delightful lady from Glasgow came to see me and explained what it entailed. I was to be the telephone go-between for the Grampian and Highland areas, which extended from Thurso, across to Fort William, then as far south as Stonehaven.

Initially, I had to appeal for as many voluntary fosterers as possible throughout the area. I had to distribute posters advertising the service, to doctors, hospitals, social workers, vets, etc, as they were the people who would have to contact me when they foresaw the need. This would be when they had a patient admitted to hospital, who owned a cat, dog or bird, or whatever, that would need to be cared for while their owner was absent.

The requests for help were seldom straight forward and could be quite time consuming. First I had to obtain details of the owners and then their pet; was it good with children, had it been vaccinated, neutered, etc. I then had to find someone suitable who was willing to foster the pet. The final placement was also time consuming as it involved liaising with; social workers, hospitals, health centres, vets and the 'foster parents'.

All of these 'peak time' telephone calls had to be paid for by fund raising, which was a new experience for me. I started with a garage sale, selling toffee, baking, plants and anything else I could lay my hands on, before moving on to car boot sales, which turned out to be very popular, particularly on a fine day. Little by little, I managed to raise approximately £500, all of which went to headquarters. I participated in the Pet Fostering service for five years until my circumstances changed.

I had acquired two Shetland Sheepdogs, initially to foster, which turned out to be long term after their owner died. Around the same time, two of my own dogs died, so the Sheepdogs stayed. At the time of arrival, they were aged seven and nine and had always been together, so I felt there was no way they could be parted.

They were very friendly and thoroughly enjoyed their country and beach walks. Not being used to the car, they would bark all the way to which-ever location I had chosen for our walk, but were always quiet on the return journey. I could never make up my mind whether the barking was due to excitement, or a dislike of the car.

I found out that The Cats Protection League were starting up a group in the area, so I decided to join. Once we were organised and our service began to get busy, I was asked to do several different tasks, as I was always available. Variety certainly was the spice of my life during that time.

I remember once rescuing four beautiful kittens, about

six weeks old from the bottom of a skip in a fish yard. I had to make a ladder out of fish boxes in order to get into the skip, which was full of, five gallon oil cans, broken glass, wire, earth, wood, and a miscellaneous assortment of other rubbish. The kittens were obviously frightened, so moved from corner to corner, hiding under yet more debris, but I finally caught two, one in each hand.

The problem then was how to get out of the skip! For a person of small stature, holding two far from happy kittens, that presented quite an obstacle, so I shouted loudly for help, which came, in the form of workers from the yard, who hauled both me and the kittens out, without, I felt, the appropriate ceremony due to a fearless kitten rescuer!

These two were popped into a waiting basket, then I clambered back into the skip to get the other two, despite frantic burrowing on my part, the fourth kitten totally eluded me, so I settled for the three for now, determining to return for the fourth later. The elusive female kitten was finally found the following day.

I then made an attempt to catch the mother in order that we could get her neutered, to prevent any more 'accidental' pregnancies but she was a better escape artist than Houdini and was not going to be trapped by the likes of me! A further attempt was made a few months later when she was trapped in a workshop, but she escaped us again, oh well, you can't win them all!

On another occasion, I was called to a farm where initially, cats had been dumped and subsequently had bred, so the place was now over-run with felines of all colours and sizes. I went every fortnight for ages afterwards and was only ever successful in managing to trap four at a time. I only achieved that by starving them for twenty four hours, before they got desperate enough to enter traps baited with tasty food. The noise of the traps made the other cats wary for future visits, so although I would sit for hours observing them through a window, before attempting to trap them, more often than not, I would come away empty handed.

We had to ensure that we had suitable homes available for any cats that we did trap, after they had been taken to the Vets to be neutered. When the cats arrived in their new homes, they were housed in a shed or a loft from where they couldn't escape, for a period of approximately three weeks, in order that they would accept their new environment.

When the lady who owned the farm retired a few months later, we returned with re-inforcements from another organisation in order to ensure that we caught all the remaining cats. At the end of the day, we counted a total of thirty five cats and kittens, every one of which was successfully re-homed.

As with the Pet Fostering service, fund raising was another important function for the group as food bills and veterinary expenses were obviously high. This meant Jumble Sales, Spring and Autumn Fayres and various other events needed to be organised to raise enough money to ensure that the work could carry on.

In 1989, I reached the grand old age of sixty, which, to most people meant a pension, bus passes, etc, but to me, it meant that the fees for evening classes would be greatly reduced and I resolved to take every advantage of the opportunity to expand on my learning!

Eventually, after much deliberation, I chose Painting, for no other reason, but that I quite fancied the idea even though I hadn't done any 'brush' work of the artistic kind since I was at school, forty six years previously. I thoroughly enjoyed the evening out at the enrolment session and finally chose a course in oil painting, which I had never done before.

To begin with, my efforts were rather pitiful to say the least, but that didn't matter, as I thoroughly enjoyed myself and the time passed quickly. The company was jovial and the whole experience gave me an appetite for better things to come.

After about four years in town, I was beginning to have misgivings, as my heart had always been in the country. These feelings made me restless and I found myself looking at the property advertisments, thinking 'will I, won't I'. After a lot of deliberation, the answer was definitely yes, so I started viewing properties in and around villages. This went on for about a year, which included me putting in several unsucessful offers.

What I was looking for was a house or bungalow, facing south for the sunshine, which was important to me. I also wanted a big garden so that the dogs would have plenty of freedom. Eventually, in September 1991, I found what I was looking for and I then put my house on the market. Buying a house before you had sold your existing one may not seem a good idea, but I had to be sure that my new home would be just right, especially for the dogs.

Unfortunately, my home was slower in selling than I had anticipated so it was a further four months before I moved into my new house. During that time, I had a garage built and got accommodation ready for the dogs, with suitable fencing erected, so they would be safe.

My house in town was duly sold and a removal date was set for January 1992. I hadn't realised how much extra bits and pieces I had accumulated during the previous years, I had loads of stuff that other people would have discarded, but which I tend to hold on to. Among other things, I had lots of plants to take with me, but the removal people were very good natured about my assorted possessions.

I went back in the evening after everything was installed to collect the animals, then for several days following that I was back to the town house to prepare it for the new owners. This was another exhausting time for me, amazing how adrenalin seems to keep you going, then when the 'heat is off', you flop into a stupor!

CHAPTER 21

LIVING IN A VILLAGE

The first thing that struck me about moving inland, was the temperature at night. While I was preparing for the move I was returning to town around five in the evening and the frost in the village was quite pronounced, whereas there wasn't any in town. I don't like, and can't stand the cold, and even though my new house had central heating, it had been empty for the best part of a year and felt very chilly.

The internal walls were made of solid block and not insulated, so it took months for the house to really heat up, and by then summer had arrived. There was a gas fire in my living room, but I soon found it was a very expensive means of heating, as seemingly nine tenths of the heat went up the chimney. I decided to put in a coal fire before the coming of winter and I never regreted that decision as there is nothing to beat an open fire.

The first summer in my house, I began to get the definite feeling that all was not well as small cracks in the masonry under the front windows were getting wider. I contacted the roads department, they said my problem was nothing to do with them, and suggested I tried the Water Board. After many months they appeared, and quickly said they also had nothing to do with my problem and to contact the Fire Service, who in turn told me to contact the Roads Department.

I was feeling more than a little fed up by this time.

As the original survey was to my mind unsatisfactory, I sought the help of the local Member of Parliament, who made enquiries with the firm who carried it out. They accepted no responsibility whatsoever for any structural problems, saying that what I had asked and paid for, was a valuation, so that line of enquiry got me nowhere. Apparently you cannot sue a surveyor, lucky for them!

Having M.E., your brain doesn't work as it should, and your thinking powers are often not very good, especially if you are tired. What I should have done much earlier, was contact my insurance company, which I did eventually, as I wasn't getting anywhere with anyone else.

They sent a gentleman to see me, and to check over the property. A Structural Surveyor was then called in, and he told me he was often called to inspect property when the owners 'THOUGHT' they had a problem, then said with a stern expression "You have a problem."

He then organised for some men to dig at the four corners at the outside of the house, to see what the foundations were like, and they reported that although the foundations were four and a half feet down, the house was built on wet clay, and that the foundations should have been six feet down, beyond the wet clay. They also discovered water in places, this meant real trouble!! I was beginning to wonder what I had bought by this time, as you can imagine!

The people concerned, met to discuss what was to happen, and eventually decided that the house would have to be underpinned. This meant digging down six feet under the foundations towards the centre of the house, approximately two feet in. The underpinning was to be carried out every two metres, doing both gables and the back of the house, leaving the foundations at the front.

The front windows were removed down to foundation level. This was done early on, which meant that I was in darkness in the front two rooms for ten long weeks.

The work was supposed to start June 1994, but it was into October, before the work actually got underway. As winter was approaching, I was keen to wait till Spring, but the powers that be, said it couldn't wait.

When the digging started at the back of the house, as fast as the holes were dug, they filled up with water. In the end, I ended up with two feet of water actually under my bedroom floor.

It was suggested that I move out, and my furniture put on a mobile van, in the garden. I however, didn't agree with that arrangement, I wanted to keep an eye on the proceedings, which later turned out to be necessary. Also I had the animals to consider, they were happy where they were.

They eventually discovered that the water was coming from a field drain which had burst more than six foot down, under the back of the house. It was traced across the road to a school playing field. This drain had to be diverted away from the house and into the street drains.

The big question was, who was to pay, as the insurance, water board, or school board would not consider the matter. While the squabbling was going on, there was heavy rain, and the drain overflowed. This was unfortunately during the weekend when no workmen were around. On the Sunday morning, I had to ask a relative for help to fix up a pump, and I pumped water all day, as it poured out of a six inch drain, flooding everywhere around. That was the first of many nightmares.

The new lintels for the two front windows came the wrong size, the kitchen window was put in too high, neither would it open properly, so had to be taken out, then put in again. I had no steps to either the back or front doors, and had to walk in and out of the house by means of a plank forming a bridge over a six foot drop, which kept filling up with water.

After the workmen left for the day, a slim stretch of plastic mesh netting, was loosely draped around the deep holes. If it was windy the plastic would blow and so expose the holes. This was a great danger as far as my little dog was concerned, as by then, she had started to lose her sight.

A few days before Christmas, my front windows were put in, so at last I could now differentiate between day and night, and once more see the world go by. It was goodbye to the workmen for two plus weeks, while they took their holidays, before work resumed again.

The hours of daylight were now so short, that the work trailed on, and on. Corners were being cut, and I presume this was because the job would no longer be proving profitable. Financial meetings were taking place with lots of arguing, on all sides. Originally, the work was estimated to take six to eight weeks. Instead, it went on for five months with continuing problems requiring attention for sometime after that, especially with the double glazed windows as they kept letting in draughts.

By then, I was mentally and physically exhausted, the whole exercise had been an absolute nightmare. It took me some time to get over the hassle and everything else. After witnessing my garden being turned into a battlefield, my first task was to try and repair the flower beds, as they had been trampled on, run over and dug up. Some areas were so impacted that I had to replace the soil and clay. This was heavy work and I could only do a little at a time.

In due course I put down gravel and stones for drainage then filled it with pruning's from shrubs, to add bulk, before I put in compost and topsoil. I replanted with roses and carnations which I had grown from seed.

To my great surprise some of the Southern Wood which had been put in the bottom of the trench one foot down, had taken root, and was soon growing up through the roses. As always, the sight of new life in my garden, cheered me up, which helped no end at this trying time.

THE CIRCUS ON MY LAWN

From my kitchen window
One sunny August morn
The Sparrows were performing
A Circus on my lawn

They were perching on the Pampas
With its bold and upright fronds
Swinging to an fro
Until they touched the ground

The seeds they were a pecking
Were meant for a Winter store
But, for this year at least
That will be no more

CHAPTER 22

MY CONCERN FOR THE PEOPLE OF BOSNIA AND RWANDA

One morning when I was watching the television, I witnessed the terrible pictures of the Bosnian women and children, fleeing from their homes carrying everything they possessed. I was so moved, that when an appeal went out for food. clothing, toiletries, baby items, and blankets, I felt I had to do something to help these poor people.

I contacted the local reporter of a daily newspaper, and asked if they could put an article in the paper, requesting donations from people and within a very short time, I had numerous phone calls from people offering all sorts of things. Some were delivered to my house, and others I had to collect.

I quickly realised I would have to do raids on the shops for all sizes of strong cardboard boxes. This I did, to the point that the shops must have got sick of the sight of me! I required masses of parcel tape and sellotape, as the boxes had to be securely sealed and all the contents needed to be labelled on the outside.

At that time, I hadn't realised the full impact of what I had taken on, I got loads of food - dried and tinned from a wholesaler and also from individuals, and in particular, lots from schools. I went around the shops to ask for donations of toothpaste, toothbrushes, tin openers and candles. I also bought sponges, soap and baby items which were boxed separately. The food parcels were packed to suit a family and contained on average twenty four items - mainly tinned soup, milk, spaghetti, macaroni, rice and fruit, sugar, flour and dried milk.

Toiletries such as soap, toothpaste and a towel were packed into the boxes and an extra item such as a child's jumper or pair of socks made up any spaces that may have remained. I also remembered to add plastic spoons and tin openers, as the recipients had left everything behind.

After spending days packing and sealing the boxes, a local contractor kindly took them to Aberdeen where they were then transported by Red Star, free of charge, to the depot for 'Feed the Children' in Reading. The majority of goods that were collected and ended up in this store, then went over land to Bosnia. Occasionally a cargo boat would transport some, if it was going to Split, leaving from the docks in London.

After the food boxes were collected, I started to collect clothes and bedding, some of which I washed, as a lot of the items had been stored in lofts for quite a while.

This involved a fair bit of work, as I had rather an ancient washing machine, that had seen better days. I had wool blankets draped over radiators, and in front of the fire for days on end. The bedding was packed in large boxes, holding about six at a time and sometimes pillows were included.

Some of the bedding, I addressed to 'Hospitals' and I also included ex nurse uniforms, nylon overalls and aprons. The daily scenes on our television screens of injured people lying on beds with little or no bedding, windows without glass and no heating, brought the horrors home to all of us. I wondered how on earth the medical staff managed to care for injured patients under such conditions.

When it came to packing the children's clothes, I tried to pack for two children of different ages and stated on the label whether it was suitable for boys, girls or both. This I felt, would aid in the distribution process.

During this time, I can picture about thirty children from a school nearby, coming to my house in pairs, headed by the schoolmaster, with the janitor taking up the rear. Each child was carrying a carrier bag with his or her own clothes and shoes that they had grown out of. They were so proud to be able to help a needy cause, the bags ended up in one of my rooms awaiting the sorting and packing process.

The last category was rather special, that was what I called baby packs. I spent many days and evenings knitting, vests, cutting duvets up into tiny cot quilts, and making covers with materials, some in nursery prints. I also made 'cosy-toes' out of imitation sheepskin under-blankets, putting zips into then. The baby packs each had a blanket, quilt or cosy-toes, several baby vests, disposable nappies and a few items of baby clothing.

A quantity of baby milk with either a bottle or cup was packed as well as toiletries. Sending the baby packs made me feel good in myself, as I was particularly moved by the plight of the children. In all, three hundred and eighty five boxes left my house for Bosnia and the process took several months.

About this time, I was taken to a big store on the outskirts of the city, by the son of a friend, and I was able to deliver the cot part of two prams, a typewriter and scales, which would have been impossible to pack in boxes.

I really had my eyes opened that day as there was hospital beds, stretchers from the Oil Industry, along with two tons of cooking utensils, also cots, prams and a mountain of clothes to name just a few. Even fur coats seemed to be numerous, there certainly was a lot of caring people around.

In due course, the headquarters in Reading informed me that there were enough clothes in store, and they now required money to buy medicines and nappies. These were cheaper to buy in bulk nearer Bosnia, so saving money in transit.

I then decided to start fundraising once again. I raided

my garden, dividing up perennial plants, and growing plants from seedlings. That, along with bric-a-brac bought in boxes at auction sales, plus the usual Toffee and homebakes, helped to raise several hundred pounds. At that time, they were asking for donations in units of £20 for baby packs.

I was asked to include a note with my name, address and a message in with my donations. After one lady received one of these packs, she sent me a lovely letter with a photograph of her beautiful son. There was no mention of a husband, which left me wondering if her husband had been killed, or if she had been raped by the Serbs, which was seemingly a fairly common occurrence during that evil war.

I sincerely hope that the majority of those brave people, have been able to pick up at least most of the pieces of their lives, and start afresh again. They certainly deserved all the luck in the world.

After Bosnia, there was soon an appeal on television for knitted tops in Rwanda. They were very simple patterns and quick to knit. It was suggested that they were made in colourful stripes, but trying to avoid the colour white, as white is the colour of mourning in Africa.

This was convenient as it meant any odds and ends of wool could be used up. Several friends joined in knitting tops, and others knitted blankets, either in squares or strips which were then sewn. They were all beautiful and colourful, and I hope they helped to keep lots of children warm.

Unfortunately, I have had to call a halt to knitting for the time being, as I injured my thumb and wrist while splitting logs with a large axe as they were too big for the fire. The damage was done when the axe got stuck in logs full of knots. It was so deeply inbedded, I had to use a large hammer on the axe to free it from the block!

CHAPTER 23

TEETHING TROUBLES

When we are born, in the vast majority of cases, all our bits and pieces are there, and assembled in their right order, which is a miracle in itself. We don't know how they all work, but it is not long before we find out, sometimes experiencing pain in the process. Individuals may have differing problems but our teeth are the one part of our anatomy that causes us all 'teething' troubles at times.

We have pain and discomfort while cutting them, which may result in a lot of floor walking for mum in the middle of the night. Then at the other end of the scale, they develop cavities, which nowadays are religiously filled and preserved for as long as possible. It didn't always happen like that, as I remember only too well.

One of my customers was a dentist, and when he called to collect his dog from my kennels, he observed me taking a deep intake of breath, and the 'wow' effect when cold air entered a cavity in one of my front teeth. He commented that I had never gone to see him about this problem and said he would make me a provisional appointment for noon the following Tuesday.

My aunt was living in town by this time, and as she knew I wouldn't have time for lunch before my appointment, she said she would have sandwiches ready for me when I had finished with the dentist.

When I sat down in his chair, he took one look at my mouth and said, "Now what do we have here, don't you think it would be a good idea if you had all your remaining teeth removed." I was ill prepared for this statement and indeed, allowed little time to give it much thought.

My agreement seemed to be irrelevant anyway, as in my position on the couch he had the upper hand, in more ways than one. So out my remaining nine or so teeth came, with, I insisted a whiff of gas, because of past unpleasant experiences with needles, I said no to them being inserted everywhere in my mouth. In no time at all, my teeth were all gone - ta, ta.

My immediate worry, following that of my now toothless state, was driving immediately following the extraction. However, I did manage to get as far as my Aunt's house, where all the sandwiches were ready, unfortunately there was no tea and sandwiches for me that day as you can imagine!

I stayed till I was better equipped to drive, then set off for home, and got there safely, although still feeling pretty miserable. I retired to bed for a couple of hours to clear my head. After I got up I felt hungry, having had nothing to eat since breakfast time. I had some salad and ham in the fridge, so thought it would be nice and cool. I put everything in the blender and whirred it around for a short time, then tipped the greenish mush onto my plate. The look of this was enough to remind me of something else, so it was good-bye to my tea also.

I still felt a bit rotten and didn't fancy bending down to feed the dogs, in case it would start off the bleeding again, so I telephoned my helper at that time, and she happily came on her bicycle and helped me out. By next morning I was fine, if you can call being toothless, fine.

Next step was the impression for the denture, then the fitting. That's where the problems started. My bottom teeth were proving difficult, and when I enquired if there was a problem, I was told that I had a big tongue, fat cheeks and no gums!! More or less I was asked, "How can I be expected to fit you with teeth?" He tried, but couldn't, so the bottom teeth remained in their box for eighteen years.

Recently, my eighteen year old top teeth thought they were due for retirement, so I decided to do something about it. The usual appointment and impression. The prospects of getting a good fit this time were no better than eighteen years ago, so I got the option of a full set or upper set only. I decided to give the lower one another chance so opted for the complete set.

Unfortunately, the gum deficiency was again at fault, along with wasted cheek muscles on one side, due to my spells of facial paralysis. I tried the super paste once, during the night, which I thought was a good idea, but the 'lardy' consistency of the paste was horrid, and inefficient. I was then given a powder, which works a bit better and is a slight improvement on the totally inequadate performance of the paste. I am persevering, when I am alone, so don't have to speak, and remove the offending equipment before eating. That way, my dentures and I are slowly becoming friends!

CHAPTER 24

DIFFERING INTERPRETATIONS OF PLEASURES

People have different ways of spending their spare or leisure time, it wouldn't do if we were all alike. Personally I couldn't bear to watch football, but like cricket or tennis. I get however, a great deal of pleasure listening to music on the radio, especially Classic FM, which I generally listen to for several hours daily.

I find music extremely relaxing and of course I can do other things at the same time, I don't have to concentrate, as I would have to for a play or film on television. A well known saying, "Music doth all our joys refine", is very apt. Only this afternoon, I heard John Williams, the well known guitarist and conductor quote Vlademir Askinazey, the Russian pianist and conductor, as having said "Music describes the indescribable," and I thought that was a marvellous and very true quotation.

Chopin, Beethoven and Schubert are amongst my favourite composers with solo instruments being the violin and piano. I only wish I had persevered with lessons when I was younger, but perhaps yet, I might succeed in mastering a few pieces for my own pleasure, who knows?

I also enjoy painting, which I took up as a hobby

about twelve years ago, but only seriously four years ago at evening classes. Gradually as I learned the skill, I became more adventurous, and tackled different subjects, though I have no interest in portraits. I prefer landscapes, particularly with water or snow scenes. So far, however, I have made no progress with water colours, that is a challenge for the future.

The painting continues to go quite well, or so I have been told by people who have seen my efforts. I find it very relaxing and pleasurable and time passes very quickly. You have to be in the inspirational mood for it though, or it does not work.

Some women spend hours doing embroidery or tapestry, but that is not my scene, I have not the patience for that. Cooking, I consider, almost unnecessary, as I don't like doing it, so there is no real attraction to spend time in that field, or should I say kitchen! We all have different priorities.

I have always been interested in gardening, as has many people, but it is strange, you will not find two gardens alike, it is almost like finger prints, its such an individual hobby which makes it so fascinating.

While listening to a gardening programme on the radio, one of the panel of experts said he didn't like Dahlias and Chrysanthemums, which was greeted with horrors from his co-panelists. I personally can't tolerate daisy type flowers like Marguerites.

I often wonder at the mysteries and the power of Mother Nature. For instance, how is it that ten people can each have an identical packet of seeds, yet with individual treatment, they produce entirely different looking plants of the same species.

Also, where do plants like Carnations and Sweet Peas get their perfume from, as the seeds don't have a smell! Other plants like the Masquerade Rose, manage to change colour from bud to full bloom. Mother Nature certainly doesn't choose to reveal her secrets does she? We might try and copy, but we all know what can happen when we mortals intefere.

These things always make me think of the quote; "One is nearer to God's heart in a garden than anywhere else on earth." How true that is.

CHAPTER 25

HITTING A BAD PATCH

After the repairs to my house were finally finished, I was strongly advised to, as the papers would say, "Get my affairs in order." Not having experience of such a task, I was very unprepared for what lay in front of me. An appointment was made for me to see a certain gentleman in the city.

It was a wet dismal day in May, which was not suitable weather to bring on the May flowers. The gentleman was extremely pleasant, and things went as I had anticipated to begin with. Then a page in the document was turned, and the bombshell dropped, as far as I was concerned.

His next question was, "What about your funeral?"!! I had never thought that I would have to arrange my own Funeral. There were several other questions to follow, in connection with the arrangements, which at that time, I could not answer and would have to investigate.

The effect of both this meeting and later events, proved to be absolutely devastating. I was told to visit the local records office and make some investigations there. This turned out to be rather complicated, the details of which, I prefer not to go into, but left me feeling shocked and angry. I found the task extremely harrowing, as previously, I had thought that the relatives of the deceased, were the ones who arranged the funeral. Despite great kindness and sensitivity on the matter, I left the premises in a state of shock, and in uncontrollable tears.

The incidents of that week, triggered off in me, a state of severe depression. Apart from a few 'down' periods which were of short duration and all part and parcel of having M. E., I had never experienced depression, and every day I had hoped I would feel much better tomorrow. Unfortunately, after a month of tears and misery, that tomorrow never came, and I had to seek medical assistance.

The doctor put me on a course of anti-depressants. As I had had no experience of the treatment before, I understandingly stopped taking them when I felt better after a few weeks.

My delight was to be short-lived however, as I was soon back to square one, so re-started the tablets, before again stopping them three weeks later, when I had improved.

I had not been thinking normally, otherwise I would have realised I had done something wrong. A return visit to the doctor resulted in him increasing the tablets, and he advised that I would have to continue, perhaps on a varying dose, for a minimum of six months. That did make me think, I had presumed, obviously wrongly, that this depression was short-term. I was also to have counselling to help me through this difficult time.

I was allocated, if that is the correct word, an extremely kind and gentle young man, who listened intently to what I was trying to say, between uncontrollable sobs. At this point, I thought counselling, meant a one-off visit, and I tried desperately to say as much as I could, which must have sounded more like one long ramble, as I thought I had only one chance to empty my heart of all the sorrowful feelings I had felt since my business meeting in the city. I really thought the making of my funeral arrangements was at the bottom of all my problems. I was soon to discover that it was merely the tip of the iceberg.

After four exhausting and painful sessions of counselling, I still hadn't been able to talk about what the real problem was, and for that reason I decided one night that the only way I could disclose what was at the root of my troubled mind, was to sit down and write on paper, what I had been unable to say face to face with my counsellor. I sat down with paper and pen, with some soft classical music playing in the background, which I find very relaxing, then started to write.

It was a beautiful day in late November, the ground was white with a thin layer of snow, and the sun was shining. The chrome on the cars in the car park opposite, was glistening in the sun. The scene looked very peaceful and almost from a Christmas card.

I wrote, giving each word much thought, which I found extremely difficult and painful, and to ease the tension, had several cups of coffee and something to eat, then proceeded to continue writing. Eventually, I finished around 10pm, greatly relieved, but exhausted.

Next morning, I felt like shouting, "I've done it, hooray!" I felt as though I had started to knock down 'The Berlin Wall' and that the Volcano had erupted. I can't really explain the feeling of relief, and for a few days, I felt almost exhilarated.

Next time I had a visit from my counsellor, I handed him my writing, and after he had read it he looked shocked, and was speechless, for a while. He had perhaps not expected, to find my real problem to be what it was.

As I had mentioned earlier, when I was a child, I had been sexually abused. Soon after I made this disclosure, I was given several books to read on the subject from various friends.

From my reading, I learned that my feelings during the years of abuse and the memories of the incidents, got locked away in my brain, until my depression caused me to remember. This I presumed was 'Natures Way' of protecting the innocent from constant worry.

The trauma of the funeral business, had triggered my

brain to release the disturbing and painful years of my childhood, a very 'weepy' ordeal. In one of the books I read, it said that the tears of sorrow were one way of ridding the system of impurities. For months, I don't think I could have any impurities left in my system. Never before, have I had to cope with anything as bad as this depression and it's cause.

The incidents had happened in my early years, when I was too young to fully realise what was going on, yet have had a devastating effect on my whole life since, though I did not identify why, until my 'self-revelations'.

What makes me extremely sad, and at times very angry, is that because of the abuse, I have never been able to have a normal lasting relationship with any male friend. If a friendship was heading beyond the casual stage, I had to end it somehow. My inner self always said to me, "No further!!"

My one great regret is that I have never been able to lead a normal adult life, which means that I never married or had children. Seeing many of my relatives and friends surrounded by their children and grandchildren, is a painful reminder of all I would dearly have loved to have been mine also.

Though I never realised why until recently, over the years I have bought many pictures of children, even two large pictures by the same artist, which depicts two children, a girl and boy, with tears clearly visible, running down their cheeks. I know exactly how they felt, and these pictures mean a great deal to me, especially lately.

As the therapy continued, I was encouraged to take up any hobbies I had an interest in, as this was considered to be constructive and helpful. I decided to start oil painting again, as I had attended evening classes for painting a few years before. I duly enroled for a course of classes and shortly began. The first weeks were spent painting things like oranges or onions, which after a while, started to get a bit boring, before one night, we had a major change of subject.

The arrival of our tutor into the class was closely followed by the entrance of a strapping young man. Another student, or guest teacher we thought, until he proceeded, to remove his jacket, closely followed by his shirt! Although he may have been feeling warm, I thought he was taking his efforts to cool down a wee bit far!

While the class in general was still trying to work this out, he then quickly removed the rest of his clothes, before posing at the front of us! All this had been performed without either him or the tutor having spoken a word by the way, and I can assure you that by now, the whole class was also, equally speechless!!

There was nothing to do, but start painting, which was done amid much coughing and clearing of throats. The process was further hampered somewhat when the young man, suddenly jumped and then had to re-pose, after what was presumably, an attack of cramp.

After the given time, and still without a word, our model rose, got re-dressed and disappeared as quickly as he had originally appeared. When the tutor came round to inspect and discuss each student's efforts, there was some self-conscious merriment when she discovered that everyone, without exception, had painted only the young mans head and shoulders!! As it turned out, he could have saved himself the trouble of undressing, followed by an hour and a half of posing, and his attack of cramp!!

Around this time, I also thought I might have a go at writing, which I had no experience of, other than the occasional letter, as the telephone had almost put an end to the art. I can only say I am enjoying it, other people can judge my resulting efforts for themselves.

As Christmas approached, I became increasingly miserable, this was not entirely surprising, as in the past, I didn't particularly care for the festive season. It has always been my choice for many years to spend Christmas alone, though I was never sure why until recently.

Now I know that I associate Christmas both with the unhappy events of my childhood and the fact that I have never had the baby I dreamed of. The images of Christmas, with the child in the manger, tend to bring these longings and regrets very much to the fore.

Having been so down, December and January, I long for the days to lengthen. With the indication that Spring might be on just around the way, I might regain a little more enthusiasm for life and living.

Slowly, the Snowdrops start to appear, then the colourful crocuses, they are indeed a welcome sight. With the improvement in the weather, I began to do a few jobs in the garden. I tidied up a bed of perenials, removing what was left of last years flowers and leaves. Another day, I planted two trees and pruned some roses, it was a little early for the roses, but I felt like doing it, so did.

After planting some rockery plants and Polyanthus under the trees, which I had grown from seed, the garden started to look up. With the garden improving, so too did I start to feel that I could see 'the light at the end of the tunnel'.

Although I have had several setbacks since, which were obviously upsetting, I have been told that this is quite normal and to be expected from time to time. When you are told, that it is all part of the healing process, the difficult days don't have such a painful impact.

During the past year, I lost both my Shetland Sheepdogs, six months between them. They each had health problems which I treated with homoeopathic tablets for arthritis in both, and kidney problems in one.

They did well considering they were sixteen plus and fourteen plus. Despite their age, I was very upset when they died, as I had had them for nearly eight years. Though they were adopted, I looked on them as my own, and I am always upset when any of my animals die. They are my family.

CHAPTER 26

LOOKING FORWARD

Coping with depression for the past ten months, and discovering the devastating effect abuse has had on my life, has been extremely difficult. My advice to any girl or woman who finds she has been treated in the way I was treated as a child, would be to talk, talk and keep on talking, to whoever is prepared to listen, and so get help as soon as possible. It is certainly easier and more understood now.

Help is out there, please find the courage to ask for it, before, like me, your life is ruined.

Sadly it is too late for a very special wish to materialise for me, that of being a mother and grandmother, but as I am a determined individual, I will overcome my problems, as far as is physically possible.

I feel as though I have been "through the mill" of life, but hopefully the golden wheat that is separated from the chaff, will be of good quality. If I sow it in well prepared fertile ground, and tend it carefully I hope to reap a harvest of peace and happiness for some time to come.

FEELINGS

Not for me
Was the joys of motherhood
When the cries at night
Turned to smiles by day
But for the events of an unhappy childhood
All might have been mine
Who knows?

There's no turning back
The clock of time
The last bus
Has been and gone
So from now on
I'll just have to wait and see
What my future brings along

The stable door's left open
The hurtful males have flown
Left behind pain and memories
For me, will linger on